Caring and Gender

THE GENDER LENS:
A Sage Publications / Pine Forge Press Series

Series Editors

Judith A. Howard
University of Washington

Barbara Risman
North Carolina State University

Mary Romero
Arizona State University

Joey Sprague
University of Kansas

Books in the Series

Yen Le Espiritu, *Asian American Women and Men: Labor, Laws, and Love*

Judith A. Howard and Jocelyn A. Hollander, *Gendered Situations, Gendered Selves: A Gender Lens on Social Psychology*

Michael A. Messner, *Politics of Masculinities: Men in Movements*

Judith Lorber, *Gender and the Social Construction of Illness*

Scott Coltrane, *Gender and Families*

Myra Marx Feree, Judith Lorber, and Beth B. Hess, *Revisioning Gender*

Pepper Schwartz and Virginia Rutter, *The Gender of Sexuality: Exploring Sexual Possibilities*

Francesca M. Cancian and Stacey J. Oliker, *Caring and Gender*

Books Forthcoming

Patricia Yancey Martin and David Collinson, *The Gendered Organization*

Caring and Gender

Francesca M. Cancian

University of California, Irvine

Stacey J. Oliker

University of Wisconsin, Milwaukee

PINE FORGE PRESS

Thousand Oaks ■ London ■ New Delhi

For information:

 Pine Forge Press
A Sage Publications Company
2455 Teller Road
Thousand Oaks, California 91320
E-mail: sales@pfp.sagepub.com

SAGE Publications Ltd.
6 Bonhill Street
London EC2A 4PU
United Kingdom

SAGE Publications India Pvt. Ltd.
M-32 Market
Greater Kailash I
New Delhi 110 048 India

Printed in the United States of America

Library of Congress Cataloging-in-Publication Data

Cancian, Francesca M.
  Caring and Gender / by Francesca M. Cancian and Stacey J. Oliker.
  p. cm. — (Gender lens)
  Includes bibliographical references and index.
  ISBN 0-7619-8686-3 (cloth)
  ISBN 0-8039-9096-0 (pbk.)
  1. Aged—Care—United States. 2. Caregivers—United States. 3.
Sex role—United States. 4. Aged—United States—Family
relationships. I. Oliker, Stacey. II. Title. III. Series.
  HV1461 .C355 1999
  362.6—dc21   99-6311

00 01 02 03 04 05 10 9 8 7 6 5 4 3 2 1

Production Editor:	Wendy Westgate
Production Assistant:	Nevair Kabakian
Typesetter:	Danielle Dillahunt
Indexer:	Molly Hall
Cover Designer:	Ravi Balasuriya

*To Sam's Grandmothers, Ruth Oliker and Ruth Friedland,
and to Frank Cancian and Michael Gonzales*

CONTENTS

Series Editors' Introduction   xi

Preface   xiii

Acknowledgments   xv

CHAPTER 1

Caring and Gender   **1**

What Is Caring?   2

Why Study Caring and Gender?   3

Women's Caregiving in Families: Natural or Social?   5

The Devaluation of Caregiving   9

Caregiving and Inequality   10

Plan of the Book   11

CHAPTER 2

Historical Glimpses   **13**

Colonial Contrasts   14

Work and Care Become "Separate Spheres"   21

"Every Woman Is a Nurse":
    Caregiving Becomes a Profession   27

Conclusion   35

CHAPTER 3

Caring in Families **37**

Families That Are Not Self-Sufficient 39
Parental Care for Children 45
Caring in Couples 58
Conflicts Between Paid Work and Family Caring 62
Family Care for People Who Are
    Chronically Ill or Severely Disabled 65
Conclusion 69

CHAPTER 4

Paid Caregiving **71**

Obstacles to Good Paid Care:
    Devaluing Caring, Profit-Making,
    Bureaucracy, and Hierarchy 72
Paid Care Can Be Good Care 74
Undermining the Quality of Paid Care:
    The Example of Nursing Homes 76
Separate, Gendered Spheres and
    the Devaluation of Caring 87
Caregivers' Autonomy and Nonmedical
    Standards of Care: Case Studies of Good Paid Care 91
The Care Receiver's Power 98
Conclusion 99

CHAPTER 5

Governing Care **101**

How Do Governments Support Care? 101
Gender, Care, and Welfare in the United States 105
Government and Caregiving in
    Other Industrial Countries 114
The Threat of "Big Brother" 121

How Can Government Both Support
    Caregiving and Promote Gender Equality?   127
Conclusion   133

CHAPTER 6

Caregiving in Communities   135

What Is Community Care?   136
What Are the Benefits of Care in Communities?   137
What Are the Limits of Caregiving in Communities?   141
Conclusion   148

CHAPTER 7

The Future of Caregiving   149

Explaining Gendered Caring and Gender Inequality   150
Paths to Expanding Care and Gender Equality   152

Notes and References   161
Index   178
About the Authors   183

This book provides a provocative look at one of the most important but often ignored aspects of human societies—caring. All of us sometimes take for granted the planning, sweat, and worry that go into the often invisible work of caregiving. Caregiving involves caring about and caring for others: the physical care such as bathing and feeding a child or invalid, and the emotional care of monitoring feelings and relationships. One of the most important functions of this book is to make visible the hard work of caring and to show the similarity of tasks, whether the work is done in the home, in the hospital, or at the day care center.

What makes this book unique, and relevant to courses on family, nursing, gender, and public policy, is that it uses a *gender lens* to understand the work of caregiving in contemporary societies. Cancian and Oliker show forcefully that caregiving is systematically defined as women's work in our society. And when men do caregiving, it is often quite different from the kind and tenor of caregiving provided by women. A gender lens is crucial for understanding why mothers but not fathers are usually children's primary caregivers, why nurses and physicians provide different kinds of medical services, and why government old age benefits don't apply to the work of mothering the next generation.

Caregiving is not only usually relegated to women but is often presumed to be what women do "naturally" and so is seen as instinctual rather than skilled labor, to be devalued and so poorly paid. The authors compare a "natural" theory of caregiving with a feminist sociological perspective. This book provides a social history of how women became society's caregivers and how specializing in caregiving has the unintended consequence of contributing to women's inequality.

The complex connections between gender and care have changed over time and social context. One of the major strengths of the analyses presented here is that the social organization of caregiving is compared across historical time. The book illustrates how the belief that caregiving is "natural" developed and how such a belief influences what women and men do and feel as caregivers. Caregiving in families, nursing homes, and the larger community is addressed. The book graphically shows how families are less self-sufficient than many of us would like to believe and how nurse's aides struggle to care for elderly persons in nursing homes, often without the institutional support they need. Community programs and government policies, and the implicit assumptions about gender that underlie them, are also critiqued in the pages that follow.

These analyses of the complex links between gender and caring will be of interest to anyone interested in contemporary social life. The linkages the authors make between their gendered analysis of caregiving and the appropriate social policies to address current inequities make this book particularly important for students interested in sociology, family studies, any of the social service professions (particularly nursing or social work), and—of course—for women's studies students interested in gender itself. We can all learn much about our own lives, as well caring and gender, from this powerful and insightful book.

Judith A. Howard
Barbara Risman
Mary Romero
Joey Sprague
Series Editors

Why read a book about caring? Patterns of caring and gender might seem obvious—it's what women do with their children and others in need of personal attention. It's a natural disposition, not a changeable social relationship that social scientists ought to study. Or caregiving might seem unimportant, compared to "hard core" issues like gender inequality, the changing family, the structure of the workplace, or government policies.

This book challenges the ways we take caregiving for granted. Neither feelings of caring nor the ways we care for others come naturally. We feel caring and give care differently, depending on the culture we live in, the resources we have, and the incentives and obstacles we face in everyday life.

Caring and Gender questions the conventional wisdom about caring and its association with women. Are women naturally better caregivers than men? Can paid care in an institution be good care? Can voluntary community care replace government welfare? Is the caring family disappearing?

To explore these questions, we present engaging case studies and research findings that show how caring is socially organized. We examine how gendered beliefs about care shape family life, economic roles, caregiving institutions, and government and community programs.

Societies depend on caregiving, but a sociology of care is only now beginning to emerge. Up to now, we've divided the topic into pieces. There are books on child care, gerontology, health care, and other aspects of care, but no undergraduate text that integrates these areas. By connecting them, we show how caregiving is shaped by cultural beliefs about gender, and economic and political structures. We clarify how the overall devaluation of caring work is linked to the subordination of women. We have written the book to ease problems we have faced as teachers. For courses on family, gender, social problems, medical sociology, or social organization—and for applied courses in social work, the health professions, and public policy—the book demonstrates the usefulness of a sociological approach that uses the analytical lens of gender. It introduces concepts such as "institution" and "gender ideology" to explore issues that rivet students' personal concerns, such as how to combine work and family. It offers controversial questions for lively debates: What role should government play in supporting or regulating families? Is day care for children as good as home care? It is written in an accessible, engaging style with plentiful examples and stories that make complex social dynamics, like institutionalization, concrete. Its willingness to explore oppositions between expanding care and advancing gender equality promotes critical thinking.

We offer *Caring and Gender* to invite our colleagues and students to join us in exploring caring as an unheralded but crucial relationship in a good society.

We are indebted to many colleagues for their advice and comments. Gender Lens editors Judith Howard, Barbara Risman, Mary Romero, and Joey Sprague offered encouragement and thoughtful suggestions from the beginning of the project to its conclusion. Frank Cancian, Lew Friedland, Karen Pyke, Cecilia Ridgeway, Steve Rutter, Judy Stepan-Norris, and Judith Treas gave us helpful comments on chapters. Lauren Glass, Sharon Keigher, Marcy Whitebook, and Merry Wiesner-Hanks directed us to sources. Twylla Hill gave us valuable assistance with graphs and census data. For help with production, we thank Kayla Crawford, Cheryl Larson, Jan Meza, Mary O'Brian, Debbie Ritchie-Kolberg, and Jason Van Dyke.

We also thank the important caregivers in our lives. Francesca Cancian thanks Frank Cancian for love and world-class risotto and Maria Cancian and Steve Cancian for support and shared pleasures. She thanks Edna Bonacich, Dorie Solinger, and Ann Stern for long and sustaining talks and Michael Gonzales for showing the way to accepting care and giving it. Stacey Oliker thanks Lew Friedland and Sam Oliker Friedland for so lovingly, generously, and ably sharing the work of care. She thanks her mother, Ruth Oliker, for being Sam's "other mother" and Al's crucial caregiver; Ruth Friedland, for the magic of arriving ahead of the moment we need her; and Nancy Oliker and Ron Bathgate for support and respite. In addition, she thanks the staff of the Milwaukee Jewish Community Center Adult Day Care Center for good care and good lessons in caregiving.

We list ourselves alphabetically on the title page and participated equally in the tasks of creation. Although we both worked on all the chapters, Stacey Oliker wrote the chapters on history, government, and community, and Francesca Cancian wrote the chapters on family and paid work.

CHAPTER 1

Caring and Gender

Think of a moment when you received some very, very good caregiving. Who was providing it? What kind of effort, gestures, attitudes, and feelings did your caregiver offer? What kind of feelings did the care evoke in you?

Now, think of a moment when you gave someone very good care. What prompted you to do it? What kind of effort, gestures, attitudes, and feelings did you offer? What kinds of feelings did giving care evoke in you?

We begin this book about caregiving with your experience, rather than our explanation, because the subject of this book—giving care—is difficult to capture. Some people think that caring is simple to define—it is just part of human nature. But the meaning of giving and receiving care can shift, depending on the social situation and the relationship between the caregiver and the care receiver. Recalling your own experiences might suggest some of the ways in which social relationships can shape caring.

In this book we explore the ways that social relationships—especially gender—affect caring. Our approach is sociological and feminist. We focus on caregiving as a relationship in which individual feelings, needs, wants, and actions are influenced by the society—the whole web of relationships in which the caregiver and care receiver live. We explore how a private and personal relationship—like the one you recalled, perhaps—takes meaning and direction from the cultural beliefs, social institutions, human associations, and historical events we call society.

One social pattern we will examine closely is gender: the contrasts in behavior that correspond to ideas about the biological sex categories male and female. Ideas about differences between men and women, the different social roles that men and women play, and the different opportunities and obstacles that men and women face have greatly affected patterns of caregiving. To understand caregiving, we must understand how its definitions and variations are tied to social relations of gender.

What Is Caring?

How should *caring* be defined? Is it caring when a father works two jobs so that he can send his children to college? Is a housewife who tends her small children at home a caregiver? How about a volunteer working in a children's hospital to keep medical records in order, or a teacher in a child care center, or a political activist working for free health care for poor children? It depends on how we decide to define *caring*.

According to *Merriam-Webster's Collegiate Dictionary* (9th edition), *caring* means "to feel trouble or anxiety, to feel interest or concern, to give care such as for the sick." Care includes feelings of concern, responsibility, and affection, as well as the work of attending to a person's needs. Some researchers use the label "caring about" for the feeling part of caring and the label "caring for" or "caregiving" to refer to the work of tending to another or providing services.[1]

In this book we focus on both the physical and the emotional work of caregiving, both *caring about* and *caring for*. Our working definition of *caregiving* (which we will often refer to as *caring*) is feelings of affection and responsibility combined with actions that provide responsively for an individual's personal needs or well-being, in a face-to-face relationship. Caregiving includes physical care, such as bathing or feeding a person, as well as emotional care, such as tender touch, supportive talk, empathy, and affection. It also includes providing direct services such as driving someone to a store or adjusting the medications of a hospital patient. Actions such as a husband's or government agency's provision of the money that supports caregiving we define as *support for caregiving* but not as direct caregiving.

These definitions leave many unanswered questions about exactly what to include within *caregiving*. How much affection or personal contact is necessary to define an action as caregiving? What if well-meaning action has a negative effect on the care receiver and does not meet his or her needs? For example, a hospital nurse may smile at a patient and talk to him about his surgery. The patient may feel that her smile is fake and her comments are intrusive, so he may become more depressed because of her actions. Is the nurse giving care? Our general definition does not resolve these questions, but it sketches the boundaries of what we are trying to understand in this book.[2]

Some ambiguity in defining care is unavoidable. It is counterproductive to use a precise definition of caregiving for all people in all situations because an important part of caring is providing what the care receiver feels he or she needs, and different people have different needs.

A sociological perspective suggests that *good care* may be defined differently by people with different cultural backgrounds and social positions. For example, a person's relative power in the caring situation or in the society may shape his or her view of caring. Nurses and other caregivers may define *good care* in terms of caregivers having the power and resources to provide the care they think is needed. Care receivers may emphasize the importance of care receivers defining their own needs and controlling the care they get. Affluent families may emphasize the emotional aspects of child care, as they can take for granted the physical aspects of care such as providing good food and keeping children safe. Poor families may, by necessity, focus more on protecting children and the physical, survival side of child care.[3]

In this book we will show how the kinds of care that different individuals, groups, and organizations value and that they provide depend on their social situation, how they are organized, and on cultural beliefs about caring.

Why Study Caring and Gender?

Caring is linked closely to gender. This book explores four questions about caregiving, and all of them are linked to gender: Does women's caregiving in families have mostly biological or social causes? Why is caregiving devalued in our society? How does women's caregiving contribute to gender inequality? Could our society expand caregiving and still approach gender equality? This chapter introduces these questions.[4]

Women do most of the unpaid and paid caregiving, and caring feelings and actions are viewed as naturally associated with women. People tend to see caring as part of women's biological makeup or as a fundamental personality trait that corresponds to women's reproductive role. They do not view caregiving as skilled work that is learned through practice and shaped by cultural values and economic incentives. Moreover, activities are seen as caring because women do them.

So washing someone's clothes, which is "women's work," is often seen as more caring than washing someone's car, which is "men's work."[5]

We will show that caring and gender need to be examined together because these commonsense beliefs about women, men, and caring undermine care and contribute to gender inequality. For example, the belief that mothers are the best caregivers for children because of their "maternal instincts" implies that women and not men should sacrifice their careers and stay home with their children. But research shows that men who are involved and experienced with children can be very good caregivers and that mothers are not always good caregivers.

Another misleading commonsense belief is the assumption that caring is a natural feeling and not skilled work. This belief can justify little training and low wages for paid caregivers and contribute to a lack of respect for caring work. However, studies of nurses' aides, an extremely low-paid caring occupation, show that their job involves many complex tasks that require considerable interpersonal skill, such as being able to calm down a distraught, mentally impaired patient. Our analysis of caregiving challenges the commonsense assumptions that devalue caring work, undermine the respect and rewards that caregivers receive, and reduce women's autonomy and men's opportunities to provide care.

Issues about caring and gender are also very important to both the authors of this book on a personal level. Being caregivers and supporting caregivers are key moral commitments for both of us in our personal lives and in our efforts to better our society and our communities. And we are both feminists—that is, we are committed to social equality between women and men. Our caregiving and feminist commitments sometimes seem to be in conflict, but we don't think that has to be true.

Stacey Oliker says, "After a long, carefree young adulthood, I made commitments, within a few years, to marriage, parenthood, and care for my elderly parents. The caregiving has not flowed only one way: my mother has been a caregiving 'other mother' to my child. Being a 'sandwich generation' employed mother—sandwiched between caring for a young child and frail, elderly parents—has been intensely gratifying, enormously stressful, and thought provoking. In addition, my research on how poor single mothers on workfare balance work and family obligations has made me think hard about how policies affect time and resources for care. I wonder if Americans will accept lives with little time for care or if we will limit the growing demands of workplaces and expand caregiving by bringing both government and men more actively into the labors of love."

Francesca Cancian says, "When my two children were young, I struggled to care for them and still maintain my career and my marriage. That effort basically worked because my husband and I had enough money to pay a warm and very capable housekeeper who lived with us for 12 years. She was a second mother to my children. It hurt me when my 2-year-old son called her 'Mama,' and it hurt my career when I (and not my husband) cut short my hours of work so I could be home with the kids in the afternoons. But now, as a 60-year-old woman who (most of the time) passionately enjoys her work, her marriage, and her children and grandchildren, I feel that the struggle was worthwhile. I worry, though, about most parents who obviously cannot afford a housekeeper and may not have a spouse. How can they provide good care for their children, when it was so difficult for me to do so with many more resources?" For personal and intellectual reasons, understanding caring and gender is a high priority for both authors.

In this book, we use a sociological perspective to examine caregiving and to answer feminist questions about caregiving and gender inequality. We will now describe our approach.

Women's Caregiving in Families: Natural or Social?

If you ask those around you about why women are society's main caregivers, you will probably hear two views on the subject. The first— and probably the most frequent—view you will hear is that care comes naturally to women. The second is that society somehow makes caregiving women's responsibility.

Nature as an Explanation

The conventional explanation, which we call the natural or biological perspective, is that caregiving by women in families stems from biological sex differences and the deep-seated psychological differences between men and women that develop in early childhood. These may be differences in brain chemistry or hormones, evolutionary differences between males and females, or psychological differences that correspond to reproductive biology.[6]

The natural perspective explains that caring comes from inside an individual, not from the outside social situation. Normal females have the hormones or instincts that make them good providers of hands-on physical and emotional care; most men do not. Males have the hormones and instincts to be good providers of economic support; within a family, they can tame their natural aggressiveness and become protective, loving husbands and fathers.

Natural explanations about gendered care are usually linked to an explanation of why the self-sufficient nuclear family is the ideal site of caregiving: Because of men's and women's different but complementary natures, the heterosexual, nuclear family is the natural site of caregiving, the unit best suited for giving care. Good caregiving depends on women doing what comes naturally to them as mothers, wives, and daughters, supported by breadwinning men doing what comes naturally as husbands and fathers. Good care does not depend on cultural beliefs about gender and care or on the training, money, and social services available for caregivers. The meaning of *good care* is obvious—it is what women do when they are best expressing their maternal feelings and what men do when they are providing for their family. *Bad care* is the result of bad women or perverse social institutions that undermine the family and lead women and men away from their proper roles.

Social Explanations

Instead of starting with instincts and inborn traits, the sociological perspective explores how ideals and practices of caregiving are shaped by social experiences throughout the life cycle, such as how people make a living and what they have learned about gender differences. Even though the feeling of caring about someone or the desire to give care is "inside" the caregiver, these feelings and motives for caring come from relations with others around us and our participation in social groups and institutions.

In contrast with natural explanations, a sociological perspective leads us to examine how caregiving is shaped by particular social patterns such as cultural ideals of care or economic opportunities for women and men caregivers. Men or women will tend to be good caregivers if caring confirms their identity as a "real man" or a "good woman" and if it fits prevailing cultural beliefs about gender. Men or women will focus on caregiving instead of alternative activities they know about if caring seems morally better than other activities or seems to provide more respect from others and more money, happiness, or other rewards. Men or women will also be effective caregivers if they have adequate resources of time and money and if they have learned appropriate skills and standards of caring.

Although we believe that social explanations are more useful for understanding caring than natural explanations, we recognize that the biology of human beings is one important component of caregiving. Thus, social patterns of caring have to deal with the biological facts that infants and young children need intensive, long-term care if they are to survive and that people who are very sick require the care of others. Still, we challenge the use of biology to justify conventional beliefs about caring.

Caregiving in Different Times and Places

Looking at how caregiving changes in different historical periods and social settings clarifies the usefulness of a social, as opposed to a natural, explanation. In this book, we consider how caring varies over time and across groups with different histories and cultures and different levels of wealth, prestige, and power. We also look at the economic and social costs and rewards of caregiving in different times and places. In the next chapter, for example, we encounter some startling modes of parenting when we look back in time.

A sociological perspective suggests that major social and historical changes may change ways of parenting. On the other hand, if mothering and fathering are shaped mostly by biological instincts, then relations between parents and children should remain fairly similar, despite social change.

As sociologists, we expect social institutions—the ways we organize the economy, family life, education, and government—to be especially important in shaping caregiving. *Social institutions* refers to the organizations and to the routine behaviors, incentives, and taken-for-granted beliefs and practices that make up expected ways of doing things.[7] For example, as we discuss in Chapter 2, in the nineteenth century, businesses and farms shifted from a household economy (in which women and men worked together) to an industrial economy (in which men worked for money away from the household while most women continued their work at home). This change in the economy reshaped other social institutions, such as the family and government, and changed beliefs about "natural" ways of caring.

By examining how we have come to organize caring and gender in the United States today, we show that contemporary ideals and practices of caring are not the only possibilities; they are not the natural ways; they may not be the best ways.

Historical Roots of Contemporary Caring: "Separate Spheres"

A set of beliefs that developed over a century ago, which we refer to as the ideology of "separate spheres," is especially important in clarifying why the United States organizes caring and gender the way it does. This set of beliefs took shape as the United States became a modern, industrial society. It asserts that the private sphere of family caregiving is completely separated from the public sphere of work and government. The private sphere of family relations is women's domain and requires the natural qualities of women, such as being emotional and putting the needs of others first. The public sphere is men's domain and requires men's impersonal and naturally competitive orientation. Thus caregiving should be left to women in families because the harsh, impersonal public sphere is not suited to caregiving.

As we show in the next chapter, these beliefs have not always been part of our culture. They grew in the nineteenth century and became vastly influential. This book shows how they continue to shape family patterns, citizens' rights, and workplace arrangements in ways that limit the quality of caregiving as well as men's and women's choices about earning and caring in the present.[8]

The ideology of separate spheres also affects contemporary politics and social policies. In current debates about "family values" or "family-friendly policies," we can trace how explanations and beliefs about care become translated into moral and political causes. For example, beliefs about separate spheres and natural explanations of caring justify the contemporary conservative politics of cutting back government-supported services. If caring by women in self-sufficient nuclear families is the best, most natural arrangement, then paid day care workers cannot meet the needs of children. Only the intuitive, emotional care of mothers can provide the necessary care. Thus government support for day care is a bad idea; it undermines "real" caring, which can only be given by women in families.

Feminists, in contrast, reject the ideology of separate spheres and favor social explanations of caregiving. Feminists tend to believe that women in families are given too much responsibility for caring. They argue that men can and should do more caregiving and that government and communities should provide more support for day care and other social services. Caregiving by men and paid caregivers and social responsibility for care will enrich care, not deplete it, they argue, and will help families and other caregivers provide better care.[9]

In today's debates about social problems—whether in conservative and progressive politics, in diverse religious teachings, or in everyday conversations about morality—we can hear how differing beliefs about gender and families and different explanations of caregiving become live influences in society.

The Devaluation of Caregiving

Caring is highly valued in American culture in some ways and devalued in others. Sermons at church often praise family values and caring, many people seek love and care as their primary goals in life, and advertisers use images of love and caring to sell their products. At the same time, unpaid family care work is often trivialized, ignored, and unsupported. "I'm just a housewife," a woman might say, suggesting that the many hours of skilled work that she devotes to her children, husband, relatives, and friends are not worth much.[10]

Rich or poor, parents in the United States receive much less support from the government than parents in other countries, suggesting that the United States does not consider it worthwhile to support caregiving with tax dollars. Workers who have to leave their jobs early to take a sick parent or child to the doctor may be sanctioned by supervisors and criticized by their peers. The demands of the workplace take priority over unpaid caregiving.

The devaluation of paid caregiving is more obvious. The low pay and lack of respect given to jobs such as child care worker or nurse's aide shows the worth of this activity in our economy. Most workers who give hands-on care to our youngest children and our sickest or most disabled relatives receive little training. We think of it as unskilled labor.

The devaluation of caring is linked to seeing care as a natural, feminine activity. If caring is an instinctive ability of women that does not require skill and training, then it seems reasonable to require little training for (female) caregivers such as child care workers and to pay them low wages and give them little respect.

In the next chapter, we will show how the training of nurses was blocked for many years by doctors who argued that caring for the sick comes naturally to women and does not require special knowledge. Other chapters will explore how the devaluation and lack of support for family caregiving have negative effects on women's income, leisure time, and well-being, as well as on the quality of care in society. We will examine the costs of caregiving to the women (and sometimes men) who do this work, as well as looking at the rewards of caring. Challenging the assumption that caring is women's natural role, we will try to identify the social experiences in childhood and adulthood that lead women or men to be good caregivers.

Caregiving and Inequality

The devaluation of caring is linked to the devaluation of women. Using our sociological perspective, we ask some feminist questions about caring and gender inequality: How are patterns of caregiving related to inequalities between women and men in power, prestige, and economic resources? Does women's continuing responsibility for childcare and housework give men economic advantages in the workplace and husbands power advantages at home? We also consider power relations between caregivers and care receivers and between paid caregivers and their supervisors. We examine how caregiving affects power relations and how unequal power relations affect the quality of care.[11]

We also examine the connections between gender inequality and other social hierarchies, such as those based on social class, race, and ethnicity. For example, the lowest-paid caregiving jobs, like nurses' aides, tend to be filled by women of color and by immigrants. Women who are defined as inferior because of their race or ethnicity seem to be channeled into low-prestige and low-paid "women's work" like cleaning and feeding sick people. This is one reason that caring is devalued: The work of high-status people is typically seen as more important and prestigious than the work of low-status people.[12]

Definitions of good care are also related to inequality. The dominant beliefs in a society tend to reflect the beliefs of dominant groups, according to the sociological perspective. Thus conventional definitions of care will often favor the interests of the powerful and privileged. We consider how conventional concepts of good care might emphasize the interests and lifestyles of more affluent people over the poor, how they favor the point of view of professional caregivers over low-paid care-givers and care receivers, and how they favor the interests of men over women.[13]

In the following chapters, we use our feminist sociological perspective to explore paid and unpaid caregiving for children and the ill or disabled, for healthy adults, and among people of varied times and places. Our examples are individual families, day care centers, hospitals, and community groups.

Plan of the Book

This book begins by looking at some historical changes in caregiving and then explores caregiving within the institutional settings of family, economy, government, and the community.

The next chapter, "Historical Glimpses," describes caregiving in different kinds of colonial and nineteenth-century families. We explore the historical roots of contemporary ideas about caring and gender. We also explore the development of nursing as an example of the growth of caregiving professions.

Chapter 3, "Caring in Families," examines parenting by women and men, caring in couples, and family care for the frail elderly and the chronically ill. We show how family caregiving often depends on support from relatives and others, contradicting the cultural ideal of the self-sufficient nuclear family. We also consider why women remain the primary caregivers in families, even though ideas about gender roles have changed.

In Chapter 4, "Paid Caregiving," we show how paid caring is affected by cost cutting, bureaucracy, and the devaluation of emotional care. We ask the question, Can paid care can be responsive and effective care? Using real nursing homes, hospitals, and child care centers as examples, we consider the kinds of training, working conditions, and job ladders that lead to good and bad paid care.

Then, in Chapter 5, "Governing Care," we compare government support for caregiving in the United States with other countries, examine the influence of ideas about gender and family on government programs, and consider the arguments for and against greater government support for caring. We also address the question, Can we have both gendered care and gender equality?

Finally, in Chapter 6, "Caregiving in Communities," we explore informal caregiving, organized volunteer care, and community-level advocacy to improve care. We consider the advantages and disadvantages of caregiving at the community level.

The last chapter, "The Future of Caregiving," draws together our explorations of care to consider a question about the future: Can we both expand caregiving and advance gender equality?

CHAPTER 2

Historical Glimpses

If we asked you to guess the subject of a chapter about the history of care in America, we would expect two answers to be given most frequently.

The first answer would probably sound something like, "Caring is a natural and universal state of mind—how could it have a history? Could any society have existed without it? Wasn't it always the essence of family life?"

The second answer would probably sound something like, "The history of caring shows a long and steep decline since olden times, when families were strong and communities took care of their own. Now that families and communities have weakened, caring must have, too."

This chapter paints some historical portraits of caring and caregiving that may surprise you. We show that meanings and patterns of care have differed over time and among different groups. Deciding whether family caring has declined depends on the definition of *caring* you have in mind. We focus on three historical glimpses of caregiving: in families of colonial times, in mid-nineteenth century families, and in the development of the profession of nursing.

The changes in care we glimpse in these historical settings were shaped by three important complexes of social change:

■ the transition to an industrial economy,
■ the emergence of new ideas about women and men, and
■ the development of large-scale organizations.

These massive changes in culture and social structure are concentrated in the late nineteenth and early twentieth century, yet they have critically influenced the meanings and patterns of care in present times.

We begin by looking at the place in society where one might expect always to find caring: the family. We will begin with families in the tight-knit communities of our agrarian past, to see if we can chart a decline in caregiving from the preindustrial past to the postindustrial present.

Colonial Contrasts

A look backwards to our colonial past may disrupt some images we hold of families in past times. Let us take some brief glimpses of family life among three groups: English colonists, whose culture became so influential in American life; Northeastern Native Americans, whose customs the colonials considered "savage"; and African-American slaves, who, some believe, suffered a total breakdown in family life. "Colonial Contrasts" refers to the varieties of caregiving patterns in a single historical era. It also refers to the way historical evidence contrasts with our stereotypes of caregiving in the past and challenges our convictions about what is natural or biologically fixed and what is social in origin.

Care in Colonial Families

Do you picture the American colonial family as the Golden Age of Caring? You might picture mothers reading by candlelight to a circle of rapt children or tenderly ministering to a child in tears. You might envision fathers assembling the whole family for a game of stickball after the day's work was done or a gathering of neighbors and relatives building a barn together.

These images of caring families may capture moments of care in past times, but they do not present an accurate portrait. A more realistic portrait of the colonial past would portray a daily life in which what we now call caring was a less important bond of family life and community than were hard work, discipline, and duty. Colonial Americans did not think of their families as havens of sentiment and caring. Rather, they thought of families as little communities based in work, religion, and obedience to authority.[1]

Colonial Americans lived differently than contemporary Americans, so their caregiving also was different. For one thing, colonial men and women shared both economic production and child rearing.

According to historian John Demos, the colonial family "was, first and foremost, a community of work." Poor or prosperous, families in the agrarian past were units of economic cooperation.[2] In most families, men, women, and even children were important contributors to the day-long efforts of subsistence. A "good woman," as well as a "good man" or "good child," were defined by their productive contribution to the household economy, rather than by their qualities of caring.[3]

Good parental care was defined very differently than it is today. The central principle of colonial child rearing, particularly in the English colonies, was to enforce self-control and obedience to parents, God, and the town fathers. Affectionate parents feared cultivating disrespect and disobedience. Religion taught them to subject children to harsh discipline to suppress a child's inborn evil and to develop good character. The colonials would have seen a twentieth-century caring mother or father as sinfully indulgent and damaging to a child.[4]

In the words of a Protestant minister, "Immoderate Love to, and Doating upon our Children" placed affectionate parents at risk of cultivating disrespectful and disorderly children, spoiling them for responsible adulthood. Ministers cautioned that parental love could subvert the "Authority we have over them to restrain them from Sin and Wickedness." They warned, "the Sinfull Tenderness, and Indulgence of Parents, is the Ruin of Many Children."[5]

Mothers and fathers may only rarely have followed the letter of religious advice about child rearing. By the time they were adults, diarists like William Caton, born around 1636, wrote about his parents' "motherly affection" and "fatherly care" rather than their discipline.[6] Yet religious belief constituted a powerful shared culture among colonial Americans, and thus beliefs about the dangers of emotional indulgence must have limited the expression of caring among parents who wished to do good. Although no child received the allowable death penalty for persistent disobedience under "stubborn child" laws in colonial New England, the very existence of such laws tells us something of the culture that shaped family caregiving.[7]

The ways people cared for each other and expressed affection were limited by economic hardship, by high death rates among children and adults, and by religious beliefs that stressed the importance of teaching children self-control, obedience, and piety. Thus, colonial diarists sometimes wrote of parental love, but few mention playing with children or attending to their emotional needs. Few mention their infants at all.[8] The belief in the preciousness of infancy and the need for nurturing, attentive care of children require ideas and resources that were not widespread in colonial times.

Were Colonial Mothers Caregivers?

Many contemporary Americans define caring mothers as those who are attentive to the individuality and special needs of their children, sensitive to their children's feelings, and tenderly nurturant of their moral and emotional development. If so, then we cannot properly call colonial mothers caring. One reason they could not be caring, in these terms, is they were much too busy.

Colonial women grew food for family consumption and storage, tended the fire, cooked, washed clothes, spun yarn, sewed clothes, cleaned, took care of infants, trained girl children and servants, made medicines, and took care of sick family members and servants. They bore many children to increase the possibility of raising several to adulthood, and thus they spent many years rearing children before the youngest left home. Even among prosperous families, the daily routines of child care and home-based work left little time for the attentive, emotional caregiving that much later generations would associate with good mothering.[9]

Besides being a fertile bearer of children, the good colonial mother was, most of all, a good worker. The good mother provided physical, not emotional or attentive, care. Historian Lauren Ulrich tells us that "seventeenth and eighteenth century households were busy and cluttered places where at any given moment everyone and no one might be watching the children":

> Open fires, wash kettles, and unfenced streams and ponds competed with measles, whooping cough, diphtheria, and intestinal worms as potential killers, yet mothers had little time to dote upon their children even in the most dangerous age of their life. Some parents dealt with the fragility of life through emotional distance, a mode that could lead to indifference if not outright neglect.[10]

Life was indeed fragile at a time when half of all newborn children died before adulthood. The prospect of infant death may have made some parents hesitate to invest emotions in their infants until they grew into sturdier children.[11]

In addition to performing physical tasks of care, good mothers were charged with teaching their children obedience and submission, beginning in the earliest months of life. In the widespread evangelical Protestant tradition, this involved "breaking the will" of their innately sinful and depraved "young vipers") by evoking fear as well as love; in the more moderate denominations, a mother's task was firmly "bending" wills. Religious teaching allowed for use of "the rod" (p. 36).[12] Breaking the will of a child need not require violence, but it required fear and repression of the sort that many mothers today abhor.

Susana Wesley, mother of eighteenth-century religious leader John Wesley, urged, "When a child is corrected it must be conquered . . . no wilful transgression ought ever to be forgiven without chastisement or more."[13] A child under a year might be corrected for crying; stubbornness; expressions of hunger, thirst, or emotion; or finicky eating.

Although colonial mothers may look uncaring in comparison with attentive modern ones, the activities of childbirth, feeding, cleaning, and nursing the sick cultivated attachment between mothers and children. Responsibility for infants and for home-based tasks that kept colonial mothers in constant contact with family members ensured that colonials regarded the mother as the affectionate parent. Yet, although maternal affection was valued by children, it provoked suspicion or even condemnation in the community at large. The colonials feared that a mother's "excessive fondness" could undermine a child's developing character and self-discipline. Thus, children needed a father's steady supervision.[14]

Did Colonial Fathers Care?

For fathers as well as mothers, emotional expression of parental caring was restrained by colonial ideals and long work days. Colonial fathers were undisputed heads of the family, authorized by law and religion to rule over, morally inspect, and harshly discipline their wives, children, and servants.[15] Yet, in certain respects, colonial fathers were better able to give care to children than twentieth-century fathers could: They were at home with children during the work day, rather than off to work. Fathers labored at home.

Fathers as well as mothers did the work of childrearing. The division of family roles into caregiving mother and breadwinning father had not yet developed. In their work in the fields or in the workshop, fathers supervised their sons, daughters, and young servants and provided the knowledge and training boys would need for adult livelihood. Once past infancy, boys were in the daily care of their fathers.[16] Ideally, fathers accomplished the daily care of their charges with stern discipline and without cultivating the tenderness that was believed to undermine discipline. Yet, children and the fathers who taught them, supervised them, took meals with them, and worked alongside them developed relationships of familiarity, collaboration, and inevitably, sometimes, tenderness.[17] Thus, although evidence of colonial fathers' sentiments is sparse, a son remembers "fatherly care" when he writes a diary in adulthood; a diarist father describes sitting up overnight to watch whenever a child became ill; and court records quote a craftsman who remembered that "when his child was sick, and like to die, he ran barefoot and barelegged, and with tears" to get help.[18]

In sum, colonial fathers were expected to be demanding "patri-archs," but the scope of their fatherly role and the intensity of daily responsibility for children required many acts of caregiving and many contacts with children that elicited caring. The scope and dailiness of colonial fatherhood created relationships that became more difficult to establish once fathers left home for work and became breadwinners. The way colonial fathers took care of their children, particularly their sons, involved paternal caregiving of a kind that became rare once fathers followed work out of the home.

English Colonists Encounter Native American Care

Colonial discipline and the constraint on what we now call *caring* may surprise many contemporary readers. The colonists themselves were most struck by caring among the Native Americans they encoun-tered. Native Americans often shocked their colonial neighbors by their tender care of children or, as one Jesuit put it, "the excessive love the Savages [bear] for their children."[19] Among the Iroquois, for example, cooperative work and communal life and the absence of a religion stressing inborn evil allowed for patterns of permissive and indulgent child rearing by the larger community, as well as parents. Families, oftentimes nuclear units of mother and children, lived in communal multifamily longhouses that were divided among several families re-lated through mothers. Grandmothers, aunts, uncles, and older cousins tended, fed, supervised, and played with children who lived in their midst.[20]

In stunning contrast with the colonists, children learned by example rather than discipline. Children worked alongside adults, but playfully and without punishment. "We may justly reproach them with the way they bring up their children," wrote a colonial observer. "They do not so much as know what it is to correct them." Another wrote that adults "let them do everything they like . . . under the pretext that they are not yet at the age of reason."[21]

Colonists were also dismayed by the much greater role and authority of Indian mothers and female relatives in the lives of children. Women in the Iroquois tribes may have had more authority over issues of war, leadership, and the distribution of goods than women in any known society, but many other Native American peoples also allowed women greater authority over children than European colonists.[22]

Captain Franquet, a colonist who visited the Iroquois in 1752, observed that "many English children taken prisoner in the last war whom they have adopted . . . are raised in the maner of . . . savages . . . and when they are grown, they never dream of returning to their homes."[23] Captive children frequently refused to return to the colonies. Colonists blamed their rejection of "civilized" life on the tender childrearing of the "savages." Among colonial captives of the Iroquois, children and women were more likely than men to refuse to return to the colonies when offered the chance. Their lives in the European colonies would be much more constrained.[24]

African-American Slave Strategies of Care

Another myth about family caring persists alongside of the myth of the nurturing colonial family: that in slavery, African-American families broke down. It is easy enough to imagine that in a system of involuntary servitude, where spouses are often separated and children removed from parents and sold, family morale and caring breaks down. Yet historians have traced the experiences of slave families and shown us how families found ways of caregiving against all odds.

Although slave life was riddled with disruption, slave men and women frequently married or otherwise formed two-parent households. Particularly on large plantations, where there were fewer economic pressures to sell slaves, slave owners frequently encouraged marriage as a means of increasing slave fertility and docility;[25] some encouraged families because of their own religious beliefs. Where misery did not cause the disruption of families by death, and when owners did not disrupt them by selling spouses or children, slave families were stable and long lived. Slave owners learned from costly slave resistance that tearing apart families resulted in runaways and rebellion. During the years of slavery and those following it, most African-American children lived in two-parent households or in households headed by women who were aided by their women kin.[26]

Because slaves were property, slave owners, rather than husbands, were the families' main providers and authorities. Yet slave fathers and stepfathers adapted ways of taking care of children. For example, they hunted small game in plantation forests to supplement their children's sparse diets, even when they lived in separate quarters from women and children. They tended family gardens and built furniture for the house. And they taught these skills to sons approaching manhood. Men who had been sold away from their families were the slaves most likely to risk becoming runaways, to return to them.[27]

Slave mothers developed kinshiplike relations among themselves to sustain caregiving and family life. An elderly woman would care for children too young to work when slave mothers labored in the fields 14 hours a day. Or older children cared for younger ones (it was most often slave children, not slave women, who cared for owners' infants).[28] A cook who worked for the master might also cook every day but Sunday for slave families on a small plantation or secretly feed runaway slaves. An experienced grandmother might brew medicines for neighbors or serve as midwife at births in the community.[29]

Relations among kin or cooperating women extended the boundaries of family life so that caregiving was not so concentrated in nuclear families. Extended networks of caring enabled children, elders, and sick people to be cared for, as well as they could be, under brutal slave conditions. Such networks helped parents sustain family life, even when work for or sale by the owner might keep them from directly giving family care.

Customs of family name giving, that is, passing on names of relatives to children, were common under slavery. Fathers' names were very often given to sons. Such naming customs symbolized and cemented family commitments, even as slavery denied the freedom to make them. Naming customs helped families that lived separately or were sold apart to identify as family. Family naming also helped disrupted families and kinship networks to reconstitute when slavery ended.[30]

Although caring for family members sustained a slave labor force and thus served slave owners' purposes, relations of caregiving that sustained families and built communities also deprived the slave system of full ownership of a slave's person. A former slave described her mother's and grandmother's pleasure in sewing for the children, "Dey done it 'cause they wanted to. Dey wuz workin' for deyselves den."[31]

Work and Care Become
"Separate Spheres"

As long as the workplace was the place of family life, both fathers and mothers gave care as part of their work. Men's and women's responsibilities for caregiving differed, but both could be familiar and affectionate with their children and with elder kin in the course of their daily round with them. Colonial mothers were less intensively nurturant than they are now, and fathers were more engaged in relations of daily care than they are now. Nonetheless, changes were developing in the economy, in religion, and in American politics and culture that would change the meanings of care and influence the lives of men and women into the American present.

Colonial trade began to change the meaning of work. America was settled amid a worldwide growth in trade, and early American families traded locally as well as, sometimes, over a great distance. Historians tell us that although the early colonists recognized the productive work of women, as well as men, involvement with trade and the use of money began to change their notions about men's and women's work. Even though most Americans lived on farms in the eighteenth and nineteenth centuries, once men traded goods in a marketplace and brought money into their families, the meanings of *work* began to change.[32]

Increasingly, *work* became defined by labors associated with the market, and the labors that produced a family's sustenance became "housework." A distinction between work and housework, a gendered *definition* of work itself, thus replaced the simpler gendered *division of labor* of early Americans, in which both men and women were workers but specialized in different tasks. With this change, women's productive labors were still crucial to a family, but they were viewed as an activity that was not the same, and not as valuable, as money-related work.[33] Once family caregiving was no longer regarded as work, the value of caregiving diminished.

The Breadwinner-Caregiver Family

By the end of the nineteenth century, American families, especially those of the middle classes, looked very different than they had in colonial times. An industrial economy had flowered, and men of all social classes had moved into the new family role of "breadwinner." Whether they were miserably paid laborers in factories or affluent businessmen, their work took them out of the household for most of the day (often longer), and home became a place of rest and renewal for the paid worker.

Fathers could no longer supervise their family's labors at home. Nor could they retain the role of teacher of work skills: Children were better trained for a fast-changing economy in schools or on the job. Religious and moral instruction passed from the father to the mother, who was still at home. In industrial society, the father's *family* role was to go away from the family to make money for family needs.[34] Hands-on caregiving was no longer an important part of being a father.

In the breadwinner ideal of manhood, men's "nature" became the mirror image of the breadwinner role. Unlike preindustrial patriarchs whose religious *duties* (not their biologically determined natures) required them to treat their dependents with stern discipline, men of the marketplace were seen as *naturally* aggressive, competitive, and un-emotional. These supposedly natural traits were supposed to suit men, and not women, for life in the public sphere.[35]

The character and meanings of working *inside* the home also changed. By the end of the nineteenth century, only the poorest mothers worked outside the home. Most women's work continued in the preindustrial mode: taking care of children, elders, and the sick; making clothing, food, and medicine; cleaning, laundering, marketing; and, perhaps, taking in boarders or taking over farm- or crafts work that laborer husbands left behind.[36] Yet these same productive labors took on a different meaning once men earned money wages that were viewed as a family's means of subsistence.

Breadwinner was only one new social role; housewife was its com-plement. Wages, earned in the market, became the social measure of work itself in an industrial society, and a wife's housework, unpaid and invisible in the expanding marketplace of employers and workers, became devalued in comparison to wage earning. Although housework was much the same and just as necessary as it had been in a preindus-trial society, it was increasingly viewed as an "art"—a way of life associated naturally with women, rather than a set of effortful and productive labors.[37]

When a nineteenth-century middle class wife wrote a letter to her sister, she described the dusk-to-dawn tasks of running a household.

She had built furniture, painted rooms, cooked, sewed, helped neighbors, and cared for her eight children. When she finished this account of her work, she added, "And yet, I am constantly pursued and haunted by the idea that I don't do anything."[38] The devaluation of housework was a crucial moment in the history of caregiving. The labors of caregiving had become far less visible.

Sentimental Motherhood

Industrial society produced affluence for a small, but growing, middle class whose incomes could more easily buy some of the services that middle class women once performed at home. Middle class wives bore fewer children, acquired servants, used laundries, and purchased food and clothing. So middle class mothers had more time to devote to children and to read about new ways of child rearing that differed from the stern notions of the past.

"Spare the rod and spoil the child" had been the dictum of an agrarian society in which most children had to become productive workers as soon as they were able to join in. Beginning in the eighteenth century, however, children of the middle classes were seen as needing love, indulgence, and tender cultivation. Whereas colonists viewed children as incompetent, even sinful, human miniatures, children were now viewed as precious and adorable darlings, who were innocent and good and who needed intensive, tender care and guidance to realize their potentials. American middle class mothers, not fathers, now nurtured and guided their sons, as well as their daughters, to successful adulthood and good citizenship.[39]

The new "sentimental mother" was supposed to be a constant caregiver and the morally crucial parent in children's lives: "Noble, sublime is the task of the American mother" intoned one tract on domesticity.[40] Mothers were "angels of love and fidelity who first opened our senses to behold God in his works and word."[41] In the middle classes, the preindustrial model of affectionate, but necessarily limited, involvement in child rearing was replaced by a model of intensive and passionate caring. Mothers in wealthier families began to concentrate on these relational tasks of child rearing and to delegate other time-consuming activities of care to servants. Thus, the feeding, washing, nursing, and preparing of food for the old, the sick, and children fell increasingly to servants or hired help.[42]

As people began to see the industrial city as a teeming, heartless world of individualism, competition, and corruption, they began to see families as private worlds apart from all this—as havens of care and cooperation. In preindustrial society, women were viewed (in the Biblical image of Eve) as the more ignorant, unruly, and lustful of the sexes. In contrast, nineteenth-century gender imagery portrayed women as naturally pious, submissive, and pure "angels of the hearth."[43] Emotional and tender caring was now considered the *natural essence* of true womanhood, rather than one of women's productive *social roles*. Domesticity, one writer exalted, is

> that sphere for which woman was originally intended, and to which she is so exactly fitted to adorn and bless, as the wife, the mistress of the home, the solace, the aid, and the counsellor.[44]

For a husband, it is the wife

> who makes it her daily study to lighten his cares, to soothe his sorrows, and to augment his interests; who, like a guardian angel, watches over his interests, warns him against dangers, comforts him under trials, and by her pious, assiduous, and attractive deportment, constantly endeavors to render him more virtuous, more useful, more honourable, and more happy.[45]

Emotional capacities of caring about others, sentimental inclinations to take care of them, and moral virtues of sacrificing oneself to take care of others now became viewed as virtues more natural in women than men and a more important measure of a good woman's character than a good man's. The magazine *Ladies' Museum* explained natural gender difference this way in 1825:

> Man has a rugged heart—woman a soft and tender one. Man prevents misery—woman relieves it. Man has science—woman taste. Man has judgement—woman sensibility. Man is a being of justice—woman of mercy.[46]

Tender caregiving of children and husbands became the nature and duty of the angel of the hearth. In the "sanctuary of the home . . . disinterested love is ready to sacrifice everything at the altar of affection."[47] As new beliefs about home and workplace moved them into separate spheres, caregiving was transformed from socially recognized work into the spiritual and emotional "art" inherent in women's natures. The ideals of the separate spheres concept simultaneously extolled and devalued caregiving.

Ideals and Peoples' Resources:
The Consequences for the Poor

Ideals are important sources of social inspiration, but people must have resources to realize them. Families of the laboring classes did not originate the ideal of separate spheres for men and women, but they had reasons to embrace it. Given the amount of work low-income women had to do at home and their high rates of birth, employment outside the home was a tremendous burden. Yet, to be a sole breadwinner, a husband had to have a job that would support a caregiving mother at home, and most working men's jobs did not pay a "family wage." The family that could not afford a domestic, child-centered mother had to forgo the ideal arrangement and accept the negative social consequences.

The ideal of sentimental motherhood reinforced social inequality by stigmatizing and punishing poor families. Affluent people saw mothers in low-income families as failures at caregiving. An early twentieth-century social worker wrote that a mother of the "inferior classes" "Seemed to lack feeling, sympathy, understanding, [is] decidedly hard."[48] Social workers and charitable "friendly visitors" aimed to tutor poor women in the virtues and values of sentimental motherhood—and they brought in the authorities to sanction mothers who sent children out to work or who supervised or punished them in the preindustrial ways. Single mothers were especially likely to have their children removed from the home.[49]

Poverty was widespread in industrializing America. Well into the twentieth century, wives of laborers or widowed and deserted mothers often earned money at home, taking in boarders, sewing, or laundry. Although it was paid, such work became viewed as an extension of housework. Thus, women who earned money at home were protected from the stigma of leaving the domestic sphere.[50] Nonetheless, endless labor prevented their adopting the intensive child-centered model of sentimental childrearing. They had no time to coddle and dote on children. Indeed, their children were likely to be working, either at home or outside of it. In 1820, over half of the operatives in Rhode Island's textile mills were children. In Philadelphia, at the turn of the century, children 10 to 15 years old contributed a third to nearly half the income in immigrant families. Families of the industrial working class, like preindustrial families, valued "useful children"; sentimental motherhood was inaccessible.[51]

Another consequence for women who could not conform to the domestic caregiver ideal was poor treatment when they entered the public world of men. Women who sought employment outside the home, either in others' homes or in shops, factories, and hospitals, violated the middle class canon that a proper woman's place was in the home. Employed women could not claim the domestic caregiver's respect for piety, purity, and moral goodness. Women who entered the public sphere were regarded, instead, as ignorant, immoral, licentious, and uncaring. Thus condemned, they were exposed to extreme economic exploitation at work and sexual assault at work and on the streets.[52]

The Ideal of Separate Spheres
Pervades Developing Institutions

The belief that the world was divided into separate spheres of private and public—each the responsibility of a separate gender, whose members possessed opposite natures and capacities—affected institutions beyond the family. The ideology of separate spheres became a widespread culture of beliefs and customs that shaped the developing institutions of industrial society in the nineteenth and twentieth centuries. For example, we tend to think of work as an impersonal and neutral set of organizations that men and women enter as workers. Yet the forms of work life and the meanings of being a paid worker that we now take for granted were forged in the context of ideals of separate spheres.

In preindustrial society, people prepared and ate meals, cleaned up, socialized, and watched and trained children while they worked. In industrial society, however, a worker was to leave all that at home and devote full time and energy to the job. An "all-business" work day and what we now consider "businesslike" work habits could only become an expected pattern of the work world if someone other than the worker was tending to the remaining activities of daily survival. The world we now call "work" evolved with the taken-for-granted idea that someone at home would tend young children and do enough of the home work of feeding, cleaning, and caregiving to get a day-long worker rested and back at work in the morning. In this sense, the modern organization of work and the customs of the work day evolved alongside a changing family, which ideally contained a steady working man, a domestic caring woman, and their maternally cared-for children.[53]

Caregivers Build Charities and Social Services

By the turn of the twentieth century, America was hurtling into the industrial age. Changes in work and family life, the growth of crowded cities lacking the familiarity and order of small towns, and the diverse mix of cultures among poor immigrants from all over the world evoked fear and anxiety among native-born middle class people, as well as despair and unrest among the working poor.

To reform the chaotic public world, some affluent women used part of the ideology of separate spheres—the celebration of women's caring—to justify their active participation in the public sphere. They ventured out of the home to build institutions to protect children, help the poor, and reform wayward men and women. In these reform efforts, White, middle class mothers offered their own class-based breadwinner-housewife ideals of family life and gender as a cure for urban ills. They aimed to teach poor families to adopt the values of steady employment, good housekeeping, and nurturant child rearing that they believed would create stable families and public order.[54]

Public activism by affluent caregivers—who were freed, by servants, of many time-consuming domestic labors of care—built hospitals, asylums, orphanages, schools, settlements, and other educational and charitable organizations. Affluent "domestic" women helped build organizations to provide care for individuals when families could not, either because families were far away, too poor, or too isolated or demoralized.[55]

In an era before women were entitled to vote, when men monopolized rights in the public world, activist caregivers shaped the twentieth-century development of large-scale organizations of charity, medical care, and government social services. In this era, during which domesticity was considered the proper sphere for women's activity, these new organizations of caregiving became the sites for the growth of caregiver professions, the female-dominated paid occupations of nursing, social work, and teaching.

"Every Woman Is a Nurse": Caregiving Becomes a Profession

The history of nursing provides a fascinating case for glimpsing how caregiving professions have been shaped by gender and the belief that caring comes from women's nature, not from learning. Over the past century, the training and status of nurses has improved, with the growth of paid caregiving, the emergence of health professions, and the growth of large-scale caregiving institutions such as hospitals. But nurses' gains have been limited by the domination of doctors over nurses and by the belief that, unlike doctors, nurses' caring was based on inborn, natural abilities and not on expertise and training.

The nursing profession aimed to secure social recognition of the skill in caregiving. Yet, as historian Susan Reverby phrased it, "the crucial dilemma of American nursing has been the order to care in a society that refuses to value caring."[56] Our society embraced nursing without respecting the skill and knowledge on which the profession was based.

Before Professional Nursing

Healing the sick was part of women's family caregiving in the preindustrial era. Both men and women participated in healing, but male healers generally worked episodically; female healers tended to provide ongoing care and make medicines. Most often, female healers were the mothers and daughters of a household. Men nursed in some religious orders, and men often nursed their comrades in the battlefield. Up until the twentieth century, though, even through the Civil War, wives and mothers often followed the troops and cared for their wounded men.[57]

In preindustrial America, a family's nurses were mothers, daughters, and servants of a household, or helpful women neighbors. Paid nurses were older women—usually childless, untrained, and poor—who hired themselves out as temporary nurses. Mothers, daughters, or paid nurses all applied medical knowledge that they learned at home or informally in their communities. Families of means hired doctors, nurses, and midwives to serve them at home. Families who could not pay for help pooled aid among friends and family; the hospital was a loathesome last resort.[58]

Before the late nineteenth century, hospitals were not centers of health science and cure—they were custodial facilities for the poor who were sick or dying and did not have family resources. The first hospital nurses were not practitioners of a caring profession. Rather, they were older servant women who worked and lived in hospitals. Desperately poor, sometimes recruited from prisons or poorhouses, hospital nurses were despised servant laborers. Although nurses took care of the sick, their mission was not the curative one of nurses today because few who entered a hospital expected to leave it.[59]

Lacking even a germ theory of disease or much understanding of the role of sanitation in curing illness, the nineteenth century was still an age of widespread medical ignorance. Given the immaturity of medical science and a clientele of society's least valued people, hospitals were crowded, filthy, and staffed by the least trained doctors and nurses.[60]

In the late nineteenth century, cities built more and more custodial hospitals for the poor. As cities grew and hospitals spread, the development of medical science made a new vision of hospital health care viable: hospitals as centers of medical healing care for all social classes. Farsighted women saw that the need for larger, better organized hospital workforces offered opportunities to create a profession of trained nurses.

A Caregiving Profession Emerges

Among nineteenth-century middle class women who hired caregivers at home and devoted themselves to charitable activity were some who created the profession of nursing. The most famous nurse, Florence Nightingale, was a self-trained English nurse who influenced the profession internationally. She aimed to create respectable employment for women who needed to make a living and to shape a profession of skilled, disciplined, and effective nurses who cured by caregiving.[61] Her idea of nursing merged two approaches: the first was the application of new knowledge about the crucial curative role of sanitary conditions, the cleaning of wounds, and attention to fevers and hemorrhage; the second drew on nineteenth-century gender ideals that held tender and devoted care to be a natural womanly virtue.[62]

Nightingale's two approaches reflect the contradictory ideas about women's caregiving that have been part of the nursing profession throughout its history. On the one hand, nurses accepted that women's caring was part of their biological nature. On the other hand, nurses claimed expert knowledge and skills in caring and believed these would raise their status (and effectiveness).

"Every woman is a nurse," began Florence Nightingale's manual for training (published in the United States in 1860).[63] Trained nurses, she believed, must mobilize women's natural traits for the demanding tasks of nursing. Nightingale developed strict rules of conduct and discipline that would harness women's "natural" gift for submissive caregiving to a discipline of effective health care techniques. In this way, nurses could claim a higher social status than they had previously had, as members of a disciplined occupation, different from both untrained servants and trained physicians.[64] Nightingale and American nursing leaders believed that a disciplined nursing profession, infused with female self-sacrifice and caring, could elevate women's caregiving employment and yet distinguish it from the jealously protected higher status work of male physicians.

In the nineteenth century, the practices of nurses—emphasizing cleanliness and attentive care—were much more generally effective strategies of curing the sick than the practice of physicians' immature medical science.[65] Yet, this was not enough to establish nursing as a profession. Becoming a profession involves successfully claiming a unique kind of expertise that requires training and autonomy and securing public recognition of a group's special status.[66] This was the challenge for nurses.

Doctors had claimed the unique goal of developing a curing science. Nursing leaders insisted that nurses had a unique curing role to play, but to most people, their cure appeared to be an extension of women's maternal role—hardly unique. Moreover, the profession of nursing, growing out of an occupation of poor and uneducated women, had little chance of gaining the same kind of recognition for curing that was given to the profession of upper middle class male physicians.

Although most American doctors, at this time, had little training in medicine, their social class backgrounds, their social privileges as men, and their early efforts to form exclusive professional organizations all enabled doctors to claim, as their rightful domain, both the role of scientific curer and highest authority in health care settings.[67]

Nursing leaders also aimed to build a special field of knowledge. Special training, the leaders of nursing believed, would enable nurses to monopolize a body of knowledge essential to organized health care. The problem nurses faced was that another, more powerful group—that is, doctors—was defining itself as a profession in the same health care arena and wanted no competition.

Well aware that trained nurses were potential competitors for authority and rewards in the hospital environment, many doctors actively opposed training for nurses. In 1909, Dr. Henry Bates argued in a public forum, "The instruction commonly prevalent in hospital [nurse] training schools is not only absurdly too comprehensive, but dangerous. It is sufficient to almost entirely result in nurses assuming the right to usurp the functions of physicians."[68] A year before, his colleague, Dr. W. A. Dorland, had cautioned against too much training:

> If . . . a course of instruction in nursing is engrafted upon a fair general education, and this is backed up by a heap of good common sense, then we may expect to find a capable nurse—provided she has the nursing instinct. . . . A good nurse is born, not made.[69]

To succeed in claiming a health care jurisdiction of their own, nurses accepted the authority of doctors and a subordinate role for their healing work.[70] They won public recognition for their subordinate authority and healing role by appealing to longstanding patriarchal beliefs, as well as the newer ideal of the caregiving mother. Nurses emphasized the natural healing power of dutiful, submissive womanly care.[71]

Obstacles to Professionalizing Nursing

Many obstacles blocked nursing leaders' mission to professionalize caregiving, and most of them involved the gendered meanings of care. To create the autonomous profession envisioned by some of their leaders, nurses would have had to succeed in carving out a domain of patient care in which they were not simply the helpers of those who diagnosed and medically treated disease. They would have had to distill the knowledge of successful care the way physicians developed a science of medicine. They would have had to claim autonomy over the daily care of hospital patients, such that doctors' and nurses' health care tasks became interdependent but not hierarchical (like the tasks of specialist and general physicians). And they would have had to win the public's recognition of their effectiveness and their autonomy. In brief, they would have had to develop expertise, autonomy, and recognition.[72] Nurses were blocked in each of these tasks, however, by the social meanings of care.

Nurses' claim of expertise depended on codifying and building their knowledge of care. They especially need to show that the emotional, interpersonal part of caregiving—which was a nurse's specialty—was based on special, learnable skills and knowledge. Yet a science of care could not be confined by the methods of the biological sciences; it required also a social science of interpersonal relationships. Social science, though, was just forming. And the budding disciplines of sociology and psychology were suffused by the same myths of gendered natures that dominated popular thinking.

A second and even more important obstacle to nurses' autonomy from doctors was the opposition of doctors themselves. Physicians could most easily claim a unique domain of cure by subordinating the professions whose work overlapped their own—not just nurses, but technicians, for example. Doctors could have made physicians-in-training administer their orders as hospital resident assistants, who worked inside hospitals with nurses. But having nurses act as subordinate assistants, as well as patient care specialists, ensured that nurses could not compete with doctors in the areas where their tasks and expertise overlapped.[73]

Hospital administrators also supported this subordinate arrangement because it ensured lower wage claims for their nonphysician staff. Indeed, hospitals themselves produced home-grown, low-wage nursing staffs by opening nurse training programs and requiring trainees to work 70- to 90-hour weeks at minuscule wages.[74]

Finally, neither doctors, nor the public, nor, indeed, many rank-and-file nurses understood care as a discipline rather than a natural quality of virtuous womanhood.[75] Distilling a body of caregiving knowledge and demanding that it be learned and then practiced with autonomy required caregivers to examine the fiction of women's caring nature. This idea, however, had been important for easing women's access to the men's world of paid work. The notion that women were natural caregivers had justified the entry of "respectable" women into paid work and gained esteem, if not autonomy, for nursing. In these early years of the profession, caregiving could not easily be reimagined as a gender-neutral craft without threatening losses to women, whose position in the workplace remained tenuous.

Trained nurses successfully created a secure niche in health care work—a subordinate profession defined by its merger of competence and female virtue. Doctors retained authority over scientific cure and over nurses; nurses claimed the facilitating realm of professional care. Even decades later, when the skills and knowledge required for high-technology nursing further blurred distinctions between more of the work of skilled nurses and physicians, nurses remained in a separate caste, unable to move from nursing into training for the work of physicians. Nurses' claims for improvements in training, autonomy, and pay would be effectively opposed by the medical profession and also by hospital administrations that banked on keeping their nonphysician staff low paid.[76] And even now, as scientists begin to explore the ways in which relationships of support are sources of healing, the public remains convinced that doctors are health experts and nurses are their helpers.

Nursing Hierarchies: Stratifying Patient Care

In the twentieth century, with avenues to full professional status blocked for trained nurses, nurses turned to other strategies to improve their status. From the beginning, nurses segregated the training and employment of nurses who were members of racial minorities from the work of White nurses. Black women were segregated in separate training schools and hired only in hospitals that served Black patients.[77] Adapting practices of racism that were routine in America, trained White nurses consolidated what professional privileges were available by limiting them to White women.

Secondly, by the middle of the twentieth century, trained nurses had improved their work hours and wages by organizing nursing hierarchies of authority within the ranks of hospital nurses. College graduate nurses distinguished themselves from diploma school nurses and licensed practical nurses by the years of training they received. Trained nurses increasingly specialized in case management, supervision, and the use of new medical technologies. Practical nurses, in turn, monopolized the medical tasks they were licensed to administer and delegated feeding, lifting, and other tasks of comfort and bodily care to nurses' assistants.[78]

Power and privilege in medical occupations came to be unequally divided along lines of gender, race, and class. Unequal formal training justified this inequality. Male doctors were ranked above female nurses. White nurses outranked Black nurses. College-educated nurses (who tended to be White) ranked above licensed practical nurses (who were often women of color). Practical nurses ranked above nurses' aides (who were more often immigrants or women of color).

Hands-on caregiving was delegated to lower status nurses. Over time, hospital floor management and technology administration became the principles of rank in a nursing hierarchy where caregiving skill and knowledge remained unrewarded. Nurses with professional aspirations found themselves increasingly occupied away from the patient's bedside. Even today, with new arrangements of "team care" that bring nurses back to the patient's bedside, nursing care is divided among different levels of assistants, and RNs supervise at the bedside rather than performing the interconnected tasks of care.[79]

Throughout this century, care has remained an understudied skill and an underrewarded effort, especially the interpersonal, emotional parts of care. Nurses have not yet succeeded in making care central to their discipline, although, in chapter 4, we show how some nurses are trying to do this. Yet nursing's commitments to care may be further undermined as hospitals respond to economic pressures, such as "managed care" insurance, by increasing workloads and decreasing staff.

Widespread assumptions about the "naturalness" of the difficult skills involved in attentive, healing care still pervade nursing and contribute to the rock-bottom wages of practical nurses and aides, who now do much of the hands-on, bedside caregiving in hospitals and other institutional settings of care. The healing qualities of attentiveness, comfort, communication, sensitivity, and self-discipline in caregiving have continued to be unexamined as healing skills and have continued to be seen as natural female attributes.

In the resulting organization of hospital caregiving, trained nurses found that management and technique drew them away from the bedside caregiving skills that attracted them to nursing. Their subordinates, practical nurses and especially aides, still receive little respect or pay for the healing skills they learn informally and practice but are not formally taught or explicitly required to perform. (We examine contemporary nurses' assistants in chapter 4.) Caregiving labors, whether unpaid at home or paid in caregiving organizations, remain devalued, for the effort and skill they require remain hidden by beliefs about women's caring nature.

Hierarchies of Caregiving Employment

Social work, elementary teaching, and nursing—the female-dominated caregiving professions that grew out of the efforts of nineteenth-century activist caregivers—each created hierarchies as a strategy of professionalization.[80] In each of these "semiprofessional" fields, a managerial stratum has successfully claimed the wages and status of professionals. A middle stratum of underpaid trained workers has secured improvements in wages and benefits by acquiescing in the creation of new categories of uncredentialed subordinates who provide intensive caregiving and earn some of the lowest wages of any field of employment. Child care workers, like nurses' aides, receive little acknowledgment in wages or social status of the delicate and arduous work of caregiving they perform. Their knowledge is unrecognized because it is learned informally and on the job. They work under the widespread, mistaken assumption that the knowledge they apply in caring for children is natural, rather than taught and effortfully learned and practiced. In this way, the hierarchies in caregiving professions perpetuate the devaluation of hands-on caregiving.

Conclusion

We have just glimpsed some scenes in the complex history of care. When we look at caregiving in families, we find that the meanings of care have changed greatly as social conditions have changed. This is contrary to what we would expect if patterns of care were natural.

Care has not always involved tenderness and a psychological orientation toward an individual's needs and emotions. Caring, as we think of it today, was not always a central ideal of family life. It is not a single, universal state of mind. It is not a way of being but rather various ways of doing—practices that people have defined differently depending on their religious beliefs, their ideas about human nature, their power and autonomy, and the kinds of needs and wants that their circumstances allow them to attend to.

When infants had to be fed by breast, women were viewed as more caring toward infants than men were. But women were not always viewed as natural caregivers for all children and men were not always viewed as naturally competitive. The gendered meanings of care have changed, and so have men's and women's caregiving duties.

If care has differed over time and across different groups in a single society, then we cannot say that care has declined over time from a caring past to an uncaring present. Some kinds of caregiving, such as emotional attentiveness, have increased and become more widespread. Some kinds of caregiving that took place in communities, such as day-to-day helping, became concentrated in families. Some kinds of caregiving that were confined to families, such as care of the sick and aged, have moved into caregiving occupations and organizations. Practices of care have varied and changed; the history of care is not simply a decline.

We are just beginning to uncover the history of caregiving. Examining moments of care in past times, we have glimpsed some ways in which caregiving in the family has been variously defined and practiced. We have also shown how new ideas about caring shaped large institutions, such as work. Now we enlarge on those glimpses as we examine caregiving practices in each of the social institutions of family, paid work, government, and community. Because so many of our contemporary institutions took shape in the late nineteenth and early twentieth century, we will see how that era's gender ideology of separate spheres has a continuing influence on ideas and patterns of caregiving in each of these institutions.

CHAPTER 3

Caring in Families

Families and women's roles have changed enormously in the past century, but old ideals of family caring are still powerful. Many Americans accept the ideology of separate spheres and believe that women's natural maternal instincts are the basis of family care. They believe that care for children and sick relatives should be provided by women without much assistance from men or from social services. Women in families continue to do most of the caregiving, and the United States continues to rank behind almost all other countries in providing paid parental leave, subsidized child care, and other government benefits that support family caregiving.

In this chapter, we describe the social patterns that channel women and not men into family caregiving. We challenge the ideology of self-sufficient nuclear families and show how conventional ideals and practices of caring contribute to inequality between women and men and between the affluent and the poor.

In the 1950s, the dominant family ideal was a homemaker wife who provided affection and daily care, a breadwinner husband who provided money, and two or three children. Women and men who deviated from this ideal were condemned. For example, in a national survey in 1957, 80 percent of the respondents agreed that women who remained unmarried were "sick," "neurotic," or "immoral."[1] The nineteenth-century ideology of separate spheres persisted.

In the 1990s, the breadwinner-homemaker ideal is weaker but still powerful. A nationwide poll in 1995 found that 49 percent of Americans still agree with the statement "It is much better for everyone involved if the man is the achiever outside the home and the woman takes care of the home and family."[2] At the same time, traditional nuclear families are declining, as shown in Exhibit 3.1. And new ideals are emerging—

EXHIBIT 3.1

The Decline of Traditional Nuclear Families

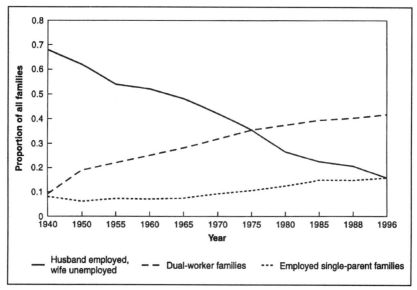

Source: Data from Hayge's "Family Members in the Work Force" and the U.S. Census Bureau.[3]

Note: "All families" includes married couples with and without children and single-parent families with children. The category "Employed Single-Parent Families" includes both male- and female-headed families. Not shown in this chart are unemployed single-parent families, married couple families with wife employed and husband unemployed, and married couple families with both the husband and wife unemployed.

the two-career family, the mother who does it all, the "new" father who is more involved with his children. These new images respond to the radical changes in families and gender roles in the United States since the 1950s. For example, in 1960, 81 percent of wives with children under six years old were full-time homemakers, compared to 37 percent in 1996.[4]

But old assumptions about women being natural caregivers persist, even in the few very egalitarian families in which the husband does a large amount of caregiving. Interviews with extremely egalitarian couples find that, even for these couples, the women usually manage the childcare and housework and the men are helpers. As one wife commented to explain why she did most of the child care, "The woman has it more in her genes to be more equipped for nurturing."[5] Although new family ideals may include a mother who works and a father who participates in child care, family caregiving is still seen as mostly women's work.

The belief that the self-sufficient nuclear family is the ideal provider of care also remains strong. Many Americans continue to think about family caring in terms of husband, wife, and children as a separate, independent unit. But a growing proportion of families does not fit this image. Single-parent households obviously do not fit, nor do older parents whose children have left home. Gay and lesbian families are invisible in these images, as are nuclear families that depend on support from their extended kin or working parents who depend on "outsiders" to care for their children. *Most* families do not fit the ideal of the self-sufficient nuclear family.

We begin this chapter by showing how family caregiving usually depends on support from relatives, community services, and other sources outside the nuclear family. Then we will look at parenting and the experiences in childhood and adulthood that lead mothers to provide much more child care than fathers. We then consider caring in couple relationships over the lifespan and how caring in heterosexual couples is affected by power differences between men and women. Finally, after describing the conflicts between family caregiving and paid employment, we turn to family caring for the frail elderly and for chronically ill family members.

Families That Are Not Self-Sufficient

Evelyn and Her Children: A Mother-Child Family

Mother-child households clearly do not fit the ideal of independent nuclear families. These families usually depend on care and support from relatives, friends, and social services in addition to their own caregiving.

About half of all children spend some time in single-parent families, almost always with the mother, and around one third of all children are now born to unmarried mothers. As well, 32 percent of single-mother families have incomes below the poverty line, compared to 5 percent of married couple families.[6]

Evelyn, a divorced Philadelphia mother, illustrates how caregiving single-mother families differ from the ideal of the self-sufficient nuclear family. Evelyn has three children, ages seven, 13, and 15. She was interviewed in 1988, in Demie Kurz's study of 129 divorced women with children. Evelyn lived on her welfare payments and food stamps, which totaled $9,000 a year, supplemented by extensive help from her parents and her sister. She never received child support from her ex-husband, and she had not been able to get off welfare because the jobs she found did not offer health care benefits. Welfare programs provided health care, including the therapist who helped her daughter cope with the divorce.[7]

Her very low income made it difficult to care for her children, but she tried to find ways to provide care with little money. To get her children presents, she had Tupperware and jewelry demonstrations in her home. "That's how I got my kids' Christmas presents this year," she explained. "They all got gold rings. They don't have to know how you got their presents—that you didn't pay for things."

She insisted on being home when the children returned from school so she could keep them from fighting with each other and could help them with homework. One child brought home a failing grade the previous year. "I said to him, 'This is it, no more.' I worked with him every night. The next quarter he came home with A's."

Despite her hardships, Evelyn kept up her hopes.

> I guess the thing that helped most of all was my children. Sometimes we would all be sitting here at this table crying and I would think, "Oh my god, I have to pull things together for my kids." It's having kids that made all of this so hard. But also, it's really them that kept me going.[8]

For Evelyn, caring for her children meant giving them her own personal attention and guidance, patched together with government assistance, help from her relatives, and assorted opportunities like Tupperware demonstrations. Contrary to the independent nuclear family ideal, her caregiving is highly dependent on support from others and does not include a husband.

The Blaines: Caring in an Extended Family Network

John and Carol Blaine and their son look like the ideal self-sufficient nuclear family at first glance: happily married husband and wife with one child and with a high enough income to support themselves. In fact, much of the care they give and receive involves an extended family network. Catherine Rowley conducted several interviews with John,

Carol, and Carol's mother.[9] Family caring is much easier and more joyful for the Blaines than for Evelyn. Their family network includes John and Carol Blaine, who have been married for eight years, their five-year-old son Brian, and Carol's mother and stepfather. Because all four adults are employed, there is enough money for a moderately comfortable lifestyle. There is also a strong tradition of caring for family members.

John Blaine is 30 years old. He has a high school education and is a truck driver, a job he enjoys immensely. The most important people in his life, he says, are his wife Carol, who works in an office as a clerk; his son Brian; and his mother-in-law Linda, who lives a block away with her husband. The Blaines live in a working class suburb in Southern California.

John and Carol Blaine are very committed to taking care of their family. Carol quit her job for four years when Brian was born, to be a full-time mother. John is a very committed husband, father, and bread-winner. When he was asked about his goals in marriage, he answered,

> I just like to see my wife happy. . . . I go about my business in life, making my wife happy. And Brian. I love Brian. Brian's great. If I'da known I was gonna have a boy like Brian, I'da wished for twins or more. Really, he's fantastic. That and trucks. Trucks is it. I've always been fascinated by trucks.

Every night, John says, he talks to Brian about what he learned at nursery school. "He'll tell me what he learned and I'll throw a couple of other things at him. . . . He understands completely what I say to him. That's the kind of rapport we have. I talk to him and he understands—it's like talking to a midget." Carol's mother comments, "As far as John is concerned that child's name is Jesus Christ."

Carol and John also help care for Carol's 92-year-old great-grand-mother, who lives in her own apartment nearby. Carol takes her to the grocery store and the doctor and helps her stay active. "Right now I'm helping her out because she's making a quilt for my mom, for my mom's birthday. . . . Last week she needed some of the padding, so I went over to Penney's and grabbed some . . . and took that over and had lunch."

Taking care of family members is a central concern of the Blaines, and the way they care for each other centers on practical help as much as affection, contrary to the conventional emphasis on tender feelings. Caring for Carol's grandmother involves work—transporting her to doctors and running errands, as Carol does, or cooking dinner for her, which Linda does twice a week. Caring for Brian means preparing his meals, doing his laundry, and driving him to and from day care, as well as talking to him and playing with him, which is John's specialty. Practical help or "tending" care is an important way family members can show tenderness and learn each other's emotional needs.

The women in the Blaine family are all involved in caring, but their responsibilities shift across their life span. Carol's grandmother receives care primarily from her daughter and granddaughter. Linda helps Carol care for Brian; keeps house for her husband; and, together with Carol, organizes family get-togethers. Carol's main caregiving job, like most mothers of young children, is tending her child; she also keeps house for her husband. If Linda became ill, Carol would have to do much more caregiving work. She would join the "sandwich generation" of women in midlife who must simultaneously care for their young children and their older relatives. For the time being, Carol and Linda share the work of family caregiving, with help from John, Linda's husband, and other relatives.

"My family is my life," Carol explains. "That's the way I was raised, you always had your family to fall back on. If something goes wrong, they help you out." And her mother Linda says, "I think you thrive on a family. . . . A family feeds upon each other. I mean give each other something. We just know that when everybody else deserts you, your family won't. Sometimes they'd probably like to."

The Blaines may seem "traditional" because family caring is the center of their lives, but they do not fit the ideal of the self-sufficient nuclear family of husband, nonworking wife, and children. Carol has returned to work and Linda also works, so Brian is in day care most of the day.

Much of the family caregiving is concentrated in the Blaines' family network, not the nuclear family household. Their ties to Carol's mother and stepfather are very close. Linda sees Brian several times a week and helps take care of him. John has become very close to his in-laws. "They're like friends," John explains. "We spend more time with them than with anybody else."

Although the couples live in separate houses, they seem like one family, John says.

> They came over here this morning to show us their new car. Carol's going over there now. . . . They'll pick up Brian and come over and play for a while. . . . My father-in-law and I own a jeep between us, and a trailer. . . . We're always changing things back and forth.

Ties to other relatives are also important. When Linda's brother, who was an alcoholic, became destitute, Linda "took him out of the gutter." He lived with Linda and her family for five years until he died. When John's sister, a teenage single parent, was investigated for child abuse and lost custody of her child, John and Carol visited her frequently and helped her regain custody. And when Carol's great-grandfather died, relatives came from Texas and all over California and helped pay the funeral expenses. "If you needed anything, all you had to do was ask. If you didn't ask, it was being done for you," John said.

Exchanging care with extended kin is critical to many working class European-American families like the Blaines, as well as many Latinos, African Americans, and Asian Americans. To them, *the family* means a large network of aunts, uncles, cousins, and godchildren and other "adopted" kin, in addition to the nuclear family. Affluent European Americans also exchange financial help and social support with relatives, but they are much more likely to be able to pay for what they need rather than depending on others.

Family caregiving in extended family networks like the Blaines' and in single-parent families like Evelyn's shows how the image of self-sufficient nuclear families distorts the reality of family caring. *Family caring* sounds like a fairly simple concept at first, but when we look more closely, we see that the definition of who is included and excluded from *the family* varies, and that *caring* also has many meanings—a mother helping her child with homework, a father talking to his son, a woman taking her grandmother to the doctor.

How the Nuclear Family Ideal Reinforces Inequality

The nuclear ideal not only covers up diversity in caring, it penalizes less affluent American families, as we discussed in Chapter 2. For many middle class and poor Americans, the ideal of the self-sufficient nuclear family stigmatizes their family life and covers up their need for social services to support family caregiving. Affluent families have the resources to live up to the nuclear ideal. This ideal also fits the family values of many European Americans, who tend to value individualism more than non-Europeans or recent immigrants, who frequently emphasize extended family ties.

"Good" fathers have to be good providers, according to the nuclear family ideal. Men who are unemployed or unable to give their families a good standard of living have no role to play in family caregiving. In fact, they are often defined as failures by themselves and by their girlfriends or wives. As a result, they may leave their families, which often makes life much harder for their wives and children, as well as for themselves.[10] "Good" mothers, according to the ideal, are supposed to be responsible for family caregiving and to have a great deal of time to care for their small children. Families that deviate from these norms are often branded as uncaring, immoral, lazy, or undeserving.

This ideal fits rich mothers much better than poor ones. Upper class and upper middle class mothers typically are married to men with high incomes, and many of them do not work. If they want to go out or work, they can afford nannies and expensive, high-quality day care. Less affluent women are more likely to be defined as inadequate mothers because they have to work full-time and use lower quality day care. The relatively poor women who are hired by affluent families to do caregiving work—very often racial minorities—will also have a hard time living up to the nuclear family ideal of caregiving.[11] Caregivers for others, they fail to meet the standards of good caregiving for their own families. Less affluent and poor employed mothers would be better able to give their children the quality of care that they want if good subsidized day care and other social services were available. However, there is little public support for such programs, partly because of the myth that "good" mothers can care for their children without help from outside the family.

Single mothers are especially stigmatized by traditional family ideals. In addition to struggling with low incomes and the burdens of combining work and solo parenting, many divorced or unmarried mothers probably feel inadequate because their family fails to measure up to the ideal nuclear pattern. Yet mother-child households are a large and rapidly growing proportion of American families because of high divorce rates and the growth in the number of those having children outside of marriage (over 30 percent of all births are now to unmarried women, compared to 6 percent in 1960).[12]

Finally, the self-sufficient nuclear family ideal encourages people to oppose government programs that support families, such as subsidized day care, welfare payments to poor single mothers, and food stamps. The nuclear family ideal implies that a "real" family includes a man and that a "real man" can always find a job and support his family. A "real woman," naturally, is a loving mother and wife who can do all the needed caregiving. Within their home, good people can create a good family. Outside forces such as the availability of jobs, the wage rate, violence in the streets, or the quality of education are of secondary importance.

Thus, the poor and needy are to blame for their own troubles and do not deserve help from the community or the government.

Traditional family ideals also shape the way Americans care for their children. We will now consider the most dramatic change in child care in recent decades: the increase in day care for small children. Then we focus on gender and child care, especially the differences in fathers' and mothers' responsibilities for caregiving.

Parental Care for Children

Family Care Versus Day Care: Are Children Getting the Care They Need?

Children should be cared for by their parents, not by day care centers. This position fits conventional beliefs about gender, children, and the importance of restricting caregiving to the private sphere of the family. However, research on child care indicates that most children thrive in high-quality day care.

Seventy percent of all married women with preschool children are employed. When mothers work, about 15 percent of young children are cared for mostly by their fathers; 25 percent are cared for by relatives; and about 60 percent are in child care centers, family day care homes, or with sitters, as Exhibit 3.2 shows.[13] As more mothers join the labor force and more children are raised without fathers, a growing proportion of American preschoolers will be in day care for part of the day. Does this mean that children are being neglected?

Many people would answer yes. They would argue that day care is bad for children. Only mothers (or stable mother substitutes) can give young children the care they need, they believe; thus mothers belong at home. Some psychologists argue that children can develop a healthy personality only if they are strongly attached to their mothers and are constantly with her in the first few years of their lives.

Other researchers reject the notion that only mothers can give good care and argue that fathers, relatives, and paid caregivers can also provide good care. They point out that the increases in employed mothers and single-parent families are not going to disappear; they will probably continue. From the perspective of these researchers, the challenge is to provide all children with good care, within or outside their families.[14]

EXHIBIT 3.2

Who Cares for the Children of Employed Mothers? Percentage of Children Under Five Years Old in Selected Child Care Arrangements (1993)

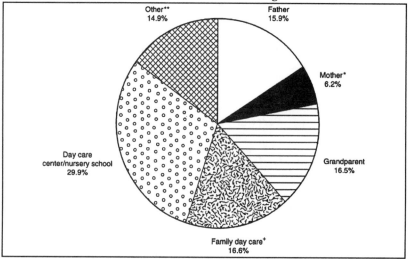

Other**
14.9%

Father
15.9%

Mother*
6.2%

Day care center/nursery school
29.9%

Grandparent
16.5%

Family day care+
16.6%

Source: Data used are from the U.S. Census Bureau.[15]
* Includes mothers working at home or away from home.
** Children cared for in other arrangements, including by other relatives.
+ Children cared for in another home by nonrelatives.

Many studies of day care measure children's intellectual and social development, instead of only mother-child attachment, and find that day care need not harm children. Home-raised children have a mixture of advantages and disadvantages compared to children in day care— and almost all the differences disappear after a few years in school. For example, day care children tend to be more outgoing in a new situation and more self-sufficient, and they behave more empathically toward other children. Home-raised children are more polite, more obedient, and less competitive with other children.

Some of these differences probably result from the relations between children and adults in the two settings. At home, there are typically one or two children who are supervised by one stable adult and controlled by her personal decisions. At day care, about 10 children may be supervised by one not-so-stable adult, and they are constantly in the company of other children; the children's routines are controlled by the rules and schedules of the center, as well as by the adult. Mothers and teachers in day care centers also treat children differently: Mothers are stricter and value good manners more; teachers are more flexible and permissive. These differences in the ratio of adults to children and in the behavior of adults help explain why day care children are less obedient to adults. Day care children also tend to be more focused on understanding and competing with other children, probably because they are more exposed to other children than children not in day care. Also, chlidren in day care have to develop ways of dealing with other children on their own, since there are few adults to supervise many children.[16] Although the exact effects of different kinds of day care on different children need much more study, it is fairly clear that reasonably good-quality day care does not have major negative effects on children.

Unfortunately, a lot of day care is not good quality because good day care is very expensive, only a few facilities receive government subsides, and subsidies are low. According to child psychologists, good day care centers should have a high ratio of caregivers to children (about 1 carer for every 4 toddlers), low turnover of caregivers, and good caregiver training.[17] Day care that meets these standards is well beyond what most families can afford or are willing to pay.

For example, providing good quality care for an infant and paying caregivers an appropriate wage would cost over $1,000 a month for each infant. Most centers cut costs by hiring fewer caregivers and paying low wages. Most child care workers earn wages below the federal poverty line and earn less than parking lot attendants or garbage collectors. As a result, the average turnover rate for workers is over 40 percent every year.[18] Low teacher ratios and high turnover mean that many children are receiving lower quality daycare.

Does the shift from home care to day care in recent decades mean that children are getting worse care now than in the past? Children are not spending much less time with their parents than they did in the 1960s, according to some studies of random samples of how Americans spent their time every day.[19] But the quality of care involves more than time. Because of the privacy of the home, it is difficult, perhaps impossible, to assess the quality of care that children get at home.

In addition, many people idealize parental care, especially care by mothers. Compared to most other developed countries, Americans are more insistent that children should be cared for by their mothers (or possibly, their fathers) and more opposed to substitute care. For example, by 1960, the United States had virtually no government-subsidized day care; France provided free day care for all children over three years old.[20]

Although many Americans insist that young children are much better off with parents than other caregivers, poor parental care can be damaging to children, just as poor substitute care can be. Most Americans know this from bitter memories of their own childhoods, from news accounts of children who are physically or sexually abused, or from psychological theories about dysfunctional families. In evaluating day care, it is important to remember that some parenting is bad. Substitute care can complement or improve family care. When this fails, some children are better off raised by others.

The Myth of Maternal Instincts

The belief in maternal instincts is another fundamental belief about family caring that distorts our vision. We assume that women, and not men, have a natural desire for children and an inborn ability to care for their children. Women, in fact, are much more involved in parenting than men—but, as we shall see, the reasons have more to do with cultural beliefs, duties assigned by gender, and opportunities in the job market than with instincts.

Motherhood does have an important biological component: only females get pregnant and nurse. In all known societies, women are the primary caretakers of infants and young children. However, mothers typically share child care with other women or with men or older children.[21] Moreover, research on parenthood shows that many women have little desire or ability to care for children, and many men are very competent fathers. Social experiences and cultural beliefs seem to be more important than biology in channeling women or men into child care.

All Women Aren't Alike and Neither Are All Men

Contrary to the myth of maternal instincts, many women do not want to care for children, and many men do. John Blaine's experiences in caring for his newborn son show that caring can feel more "natural" to a man than to a woman. John has a very strong, emotional commitment to his son, even though Carol and Linda do much more caring work than John and Linda's husband do. Carol described the situation when Brian was born:

Carol: It took me a while to get adjusted to Brian, because I'd never been around babies before. Never had a baby-sitting job, so I was a little afraid of him for a while. But we got used to each other. . . . John helped me more than anybody. In fact, I didn't even change his diapers for the first week, cause he stayed home with me for that week. . . .

Interviewer: Has he been around babies?

Carol: Oh yeah. He has a little brother . . . that was a baby when John was in his twenties. . . . Ever since I've met him, he's always out there having a blast with the kids. Goes to the beach, winds up having all the kids around him, picking up trash or building sand castles.

Perhaps because he had experienced caring for his younger brother, John was more comfortable and skilled than Carol at taking care of Brian in his early weeks.

Women are not naturally better carers than men. Many women are not suited to care for children. Some mothers abuse or neglect their children (about half of the reported cases of parental physical violence against children involve women. However, because mothers spend much more time with children than fathers, their actual rate of violence is much lower than fathers'. Still, mothers *can* be violent). Many women prefer not to have children. An estimated 15 to 20 percent of the women born in the 1950s and 1960s will remain childless, many of them by choice.[22]

Most mothers are ambivalent at times about caring for their children, researchers find. On the one hand, mothering can give a woman a sense of meaning and purpose in her life. Her identity as a woman can be fulfilled by loving and caring for her children, as a man can be fulfilled by being a good provider. On the other hand, caring for small children can sometimes be an irritating and tedious experience for most mothers, and the demands of mothering prevent many women from pursuing their other ambitions and pleasures.[23]

Martha McMahon's interviews with 59 employed mothers of preschool children in Toronto, Canada illustrate some of women's varied experiences of mothering. Rachel, a mother of two preschoolers and a high school teacher, describes her surprise at both the heavy workload of mothering and her positive feelings of love:

I had probably heard about it, but it never sunk in, how physically and mentally demanding children are. On the other hand, I never—I would never have known the kind of joy they could bring and . . . the love I was capable of having for my children. . . . I find the whole thing a miracle.[24]

Barb, a clerical worker who is the mother of a two year old, is unambivalently positive about mothering. "I don't think anything could be as wonderful as this," she says. "It's the best thing that ever happened to me in my life."[24]

However, when McMahon asked the mothers if they would still choose to have a child if they were doing things over again, almost 20 percent said no or were unsure, most them single mothers without much money. Lack of resources like time and money is one source of ambivalence for mothers. Kimberley, a single mother and a sheet metal worker, explained that without a child "I'd probably feel a little—a *lot*—better because I know I'd have a job. I'd be saving my money and I wouldn't worry about groceries." Yet disadvantage is not the only source of regret. Another single mother, Diane, who worked as a clerical assistant and became pregnant by accident, said, "I wouldn't have chosen to have a child. . . . I just didn't want kids."[25] Some women love motherhood; other mothers wish they had never had children.

Men also vary in their attitudes towards caring for their children. For many married men, being the provider still defines fatherhood; they spend little time directly caring for their children. Another expanding group of men chooses to do a substantial part of the child care. A tiny minority of husbands is equally involved or more involved in child care than their wives; we will describe some of these men later. Finally, a large and growing group of men abandons their children or are cut off from them and provides neither money nor face-to-face care. These estranged fathers include both men who never married the mothers of their children and divorced men. Most men have little contact with their children after they separate from their wives. About 32 percent of divorced fathers see their children once a year or less after the fathers move out, and 53 percent see their children once a month or less. A minority of divorced fathers have a lot of contact: 25 percent see their children once a week or more often.[26] Men as well as women vary a lot in their parenting.

Mothering and Fathering: How Different Are They?

Studies that compare the parenting of new fathers and mothers usually find few differences. One study asked fathers and mothers of infants to describe their feelings when their baby cried or smiled and also measured parents' physiological responses to their babies' behavior, such as heart rate and blood pressure, for another measure of

emotions. Both parents reported similar feelings about the baby's behavior, and their physiological reactions were similar. The researchers
conclude: "Our data do not prove that there are no biological sex
differences, but they do speak against the notion that 'maternal' responsiveness reflects predominantly biological influences."[27] Other researchers
report that fathers are "just as nurturant and stimulating" with their
infants as mothers when left alone with a newborn.[28]

Perhaps the most important evidence that biological gender differences have a minor effect on parenting is that men who have the same
experiences as women in caring for small children behave and feel
similarly to women. Scott Coltrane interviewed 20 of the tiny minority
of fathers that shares the care of small children equally with their wives.
One of the most active fathers described how he cared for his two
children in the first months of their lives: "she would nurse them but I
would bring them to the bed afterward and change them if necessary,
and get them back to sleep. . . . I really initiated those other kinds of care
aspects so that I could be involved." The fathers' intense interaction
with their babies enabled them to experience a new level of attachment
and intimacy that is usually expected only of mothers. The fathers
described their "deep emotional trust" with the baby and how parenting
was "drawing me in" and "making it difficult to deal with the outside
world."[29] Performing care activities created the caring feelings and
personal commitment to caregiving that many people associate with
maternal instincts.

Men and women do not differ greatly in their "natural" ability to be
involved, responsive, and competent parents. Of course, if one parent
(usually the mother) performs more child care activities than the other,
that parent will acquire more experience and knowledge about the child
and will probably become more comfortable with the child than the
other parent is. She (or he) is also likely to become more psychologically
attached to the child and more identified with caregiving. The child's
responsive attachment will further deepen the parent's emotion and
identification. We usually think that people with a caring personality
become caregivers, but the act of caregiving also produces more caring
individuals. "Natural" maternal caring may derive more from doing
than from being female; thus, if men do caring work, they too may
become "naturally" caring.

Turning from similarities between mothers and fathers to differences, fathers and mothers do differ in their style of child care. Fathers
favor rough-and-tumble play with small children; women favor hold-

ing and talking to the child. With older children, fathers are more likely to be strict disciplinarians; mothers have better communication with their children and talk to them more.[30] These gender differences probably stem from men and women's different parental roles.

The major difference between mothers and fathers is that mothers do much more of the daily caregiving work. In two-parent families like the Blaines, mothers do most of the essential, daily caring work such as feeding and supervising children and doing their laundry. Fathers specialize in more pleasant and intermittent activities such as playing, as John Blaine does, although there has been a small increase in fathers performing the "daily grind" of child care. A recent national survey of families found that mothers do about three quarters of the most time-consuming housework. For example, women in their first marriages do 84 percent of the meal preparation, 83 percent of the housecleaning, and 69 percent of the driving. Women still do almost 80 percent of the child care, and men have not substantially increased their child care work, according to Robinson's studies of people's daily use of time between 1965 and 1985. Some more recent studies suggest fathers are doing more child care.[31]

Single mothers have to do almost all the parental care, as most fathers who don't live with their children see them infrequently, as we have discussed. With or without husbands, women do most of the family caregiving.

Most fathers are competent at child care, or could learn to be, and most couples believe that child care should be shared equally between husband and wife if both are employed.[32] So why do mothers do so much more child care than fathers? Researchers have identified several social and cultural patterns that help answer this question. Childhood gender socialization and the lifelong impact of gender stereotypes are part of the answer. The choices and expectations of young men and women about jobs versus parenting are another element. Men's greater social power and economic discrimination against women also help explain why women and not men do most of the parenting work.

Why Mothers Do Most of the Child Care

Culture and Childhood Socialization

Young boys' and girls' relationship to their mothers is an important factor that channels females but not males into child care, according to

Nancy Chodorow's theory of gender personality formation.[33] She points out that as infants, both boys and girls have a strong identification and intimate attachment with their mothers. To become "manly," however, a boy has to be quite different from women, so the little boy is pushed to loosen his tie to his mother. His father may tell him to be a "little man" and not a "mama's boy"; his mother may become a little distant. To accomplish this painful separation, he renounces his identification with everything feminine.

Girls, on the other hand, are not pushed to separate from their mothers, so they retain their early identification and intimacy with her. As a result of this process, girls grow up to prefer intimate and caring relationships like their early relationship with their mother. Caring for their own children fulfills this need.

Boys, in contrast, grow up to be more distant and to avoid the intimate caring that might remind them of their early feminine attachment and identification. Men therefore avoid close attachments with small children (and others), and the pattern of women and not men caring for children is passed on to the next generation. This theory explains one way in which childhood experience can shape adult parenting.

Social pressure to accept gender stereotypes throughout the life span is another important process that channels women into mothering. Most Americans continue to identify femininity with caring for others and with being considerate and emotional. They identify masculinity with being aggressive, dominant, and rational, qualities that do not fit very well with the conventional picture of a good child care provider. Gender stereotypes are changing, and people with diverse social backgrounds and sexual preferences may have different ideals of femininity and masculinity.[34] Yet the belief that women are suited for caring and men are suited for providing is still widely accepted.

Consistent with these beliefs about gender differences, young girls and boys are taught different skills, to prepare them for being "real" women and men. Girls but not boys are given baby dolls to play with and are encouraged to baby-sit, which teaches them how to care for children. Girls are taught how to do the physical work involved in parenting—making beds, preparing meals, shopping for clothes. Girls are also taught the emotional part of caring and are encouraged to express tender feelings and be empathic and attentive to the needs of others; boys are trained to be tough and dominant.[35] Social pressure in school and throughout the life span usually reinforces this early learning. Images in the media and observations of everyday life at shopping malls and supermarkets confirm the assumption that child care is natural for women but not for men.

In addition to pressure from others to conform to gender stereotypes, people also pressure themselves, according to the theory of "doing gender."[36] Most people want to be seen as a "real woman" or a "real man" by themselves as well as by others. So they choose activities and mannerisms that they and the people in their social circle define as feminine or masculine. Caring for small children is so closely associated with women in our culture that women choose to be mothers partly to confirm their "womanliness" to themselves and others; men avoid child care to confirm their "manliness."[37]

Choices in Early Adulthood

Shaped by these childhood experiences, many young women have contradictory expectations and plans that lead them into traditional family roles, even though they believe in gender equality. Ann Machung, who interviewed college seniors, reports that the students' egalitarian beliefs are contradicted by their plans for the future. Most of the women expect to get graduate degrees in law, medicine, or other professions, and half expect to earn at least as much as their husband. But the male students plan to work full-time throughout their lives in a demanding career; most female students plan to interrupt work when their children are young and hope to find flexible work that allows them to care for their family. Male students see women "as wanting children more, as having the instinctual capabilities to care for them better, and therefore as having to make career sacrifices for them," and the female students agree.[38]

Jenny, one of the students who was interviewed, illustrates the students' contradictory expectations. She plans a career in radio or TV journalism, and expects "to get my career established first" in her 20s and then have children. She feels she would not take time off from work "if that meant lowering her standard of living or foregoing a possible promotion." But she also expects to put her children's needs first if there is a conflict between their needs and work. "They'll be most important when they're infants."[39]

Jenny, like most of the women surveyed, doesn't think about how her commitment to putting children's needs first is likely to undermine her career. She doesn't acknowledge that if she interrupts her career to care for her children and gives her husband's career first priority, this will probably lower her earning potential, compared to her husband. When she competes for promotions, she will suffer by comparison with others who put career first and have partners who are primarily committed to children's needs. She may find herself in a very bad financial situation if her marriage ends in divorce (as about one half of all marriages do) and the children live with her (which occurs in about 90 percent of divorces involving children). Even among the most "liberated" young women, the belief that the mother is the primary parent becomes a self-fulfilling prophecy. These choices and expectations of young adults lead women down a path focused on parenting; men pursue economic success.

But beliefs and choices made in young adulthood, before becoming a parent, are not all that pushes women and not men into doing most of the child care. Parents' current situation is also important, especially the power balance in the marriage and the job market for men and women.

Male Power

The Blaines' marriage illustrates the impact of marital power on a mother's and father's involvement in child care. Carol quit work when Brian was born and was happy to stay home until Brian was three years old. Then she wanted to return to work. But John, the dominant partner, succeeded in keeping her at home for another year. According to Carol,

> When I first met him, he was, you know, "This is the way it is. This is the way it's going to be." *I* did all the giving, he did all the —. Whenever we had a disagreement, [even if] he was totally, totally wrong, I would always say "I'm sorry."

If she didn't apologize, he wouldn't speak to her for days, which "would drive me crazy."

Carol's return to work and withdrawal from full-time mothering was closely tied to changing the balance of power in her marriage.

Carol: I don't let him run my life like I did in the beginning of our marriage. And this all stopped when I went back to work. We did have a little tiff about me going back to work. He thought that my place was at home raising Brian, and doing all that. . . . So finally I decided to come out and say, "I'm going back to work and that is that."

Interviewer: Would you say that was an improvement?

Carol: Yes, because finally, for the first time in our marriage, I stood up. I stood up to him instead of going "Oh, OK." This is something that I really wanted to do, and I hadn't done something that I really wanted to do ever since we were married. And it felt good. It was like I was breathing again and discovering life and what was going on outside my role inside my house.

So Carol stayed home for four years instead of three, not because of her maternal instincts but because she submitted to John.

In many families, women do most of the family caregiving because of men's power advantage. Most marriages today seem to have little to do with male domination, on the surface. Couples usually describe themselves as sharing power equally, if they are asked. But the traditional pattern of the man providing most of the money and the woman doing most of the family caring typically creates male dominance, as it did in the Blaines' marriage, because money is linked to power.

The more income a husband makes, compared to his wife, the more he will get his way at home, many studies have shown.[40] If he makes most of the money, she will need him more than he needs her. Similarly, if his prospects for remarriage are better than hers because the pool of "eligibles" is larger (think of whom 40-year-old men and 40-year-old women date), she will be more dependent on this marriage. Unequal dependency for money or for other things will give a power advantage to the less-dependent spouse, according to some theories of power.[41] Thus husbands typically have a power advantage. They often use it to get out of the most unpleasant and time-consuming parts of caregiving, like staying home with young children, and to pressure their wives into doing this caregiving, like John did with Carol. As a result, husbands have more time and energy to advance their careers.

Wives who do most of the family caregiving have fewer opportunities to earn money. This makes the wife more financially dependent on her husband and further increases his power advantage. She may also become more dependent on her husband for social contact and knowledge about the wider world because she is isolated in her home.

Women's preparation for mothering and men's preparation for providing also produces male dominance. Girls are socialized to put the needs of others first; boys are trained to be dominant and win. Young women are encouraged to make educational and occupational choices that sacrifice income to flexible time for parenting; young men are urged to make decisions that lead to high incomes. Thus women's anticipation of doing more mothering than men strengthens male dominance, and men's power advantage contributes to women doing more family caregiving than men.

Economic Discrimination

Current job opportunities for young mothers also encourage women to mother. If good jobs are not available, a woman is more likely to lose her interest in employment and become more attracted to mothering and homemaking. Many of the jobs available to women are dead end and low paid. Over 30 percent of employed women are in low-paid, traditionally female jobs: They work as secretaries, cashiers, nurses' aides, waitresses, and food preparation workers, or in retail sales.[42]

When job opportunities for women improve, many women are drawn away from full-time motherhood. For men too, parenting is tied to current economic constraints and opportunities. Many men spend little time with their children in part because their jobs keep them away from home. Men who leave work earlier in the day than their peers to attend to their children may reduce their chance for a promotion, become the butt of hostile jokes at work, or even risk being fired in the next downsizing.[43]

Kathleen Gerson's interviews with 63 college-educated White women in their late 20s and early 30s show the impact of current job opportunities on mothering. She asked the women about their current involvement in work as opposed to homemaking and about the aspirations they had formed in childhood. Most of the women in her study deviated from their original goals because of the options available to them as adults. Many women who started out wanting to be homemakers were childless and devoted to their careers in their 30s because they had encountered good jobs or had poor prospects for a stable marriage. For example, a married, 29-year-old computer programmer chose to postpone having children when a better job became available. After six years working as a keypunch operator-secretary, "I wanted to quit," she said, "and then start having children" because the job was boring and low paid. But then she changed her mind "because my boss asked me if I wanted to be a programmer trainee. . . . And I've really liked my job ever since, as a programmer and now as a programmer analyst."[44] She remains childless. Other women who started out being career oriented became homemakers because they hit the "glass ceiling" on women's job opportunities, became discouraged about work, and could rely on husbands with good incomes. Gender inequality at the workplace, as well as at home, contributes to women doing most of the parenting work.

We can understand women's and men's parental caregiving much better if we consider their current economic opportunities and the balance of power in male-female relationships, as well as their experiences as children and as young adults. The impact of all these factors clarifies how gendered parenting is socially constructed—that it is not simply a natural result of maternal instincts.

Caring in Couples

Caring within couples is also shaped by gender, economics, and cultural beliefs, as well as the balance of power in the couple. Looking at the daily exchanges of emotional and practical support in couples reminds us that almost everyone needs care, contrary to American beliefs about the virtues of individualism and the dangers of dependency. Individualism implies that the ideal adult is self-sufficient and does not need help from others. Adults should be able to take care of themselves and their own families without depending on outsiders or on government social services. An adult who depends on care from others is inferior or deficient, someone to be pitied, according to individualism. However, these beliefs are challenged by research on caring in couples that shows that most adults want and need care.

We will first consider the different ways that partners in a couple relationship can care for each other. Then we will look at how gender and power are related to caring in heterosexual couples.

Mutual Caring in Couples: The Myth of Self-Sufficient Individuals

There are many kinds of care receivers: not only a chronically ill older person, but a healthy undergraduate whose boyfriend takes her out for coffee when she is upset or a vigorous and successful executive whose wife takes care of his meals, clothing, and social life, even though he could do these things for himself. Most people want and receive some kinds of care, which we have defined as face-to-face interactions in which one person feels affection and responsibility for the other and provides for the other's personal needs.

Marriage or a committed love relationship is *the* dominant image in our culture of a caring relationship for adults. The heterosexual couple who share love, sexuality, a home, money, and companionship is the most frequent positive image in the mass media. Popular songs, advertisements, and the dreams of many girls (and boys) focus on the loving couple as the major source of love, caring, and happiness. This is the only relationship in which the dependency of one adult on another is generally expected and approved. Despite this ideal, many adults, especially women, receive more emotional caring and practical help from their friends, parents, adult children, and other relatives than they do from their sexual partners.[45]

Ways of Caring in Couples

John and Carol Blaine's marriage illustrates one kind of caring that a couple relationship can provide. What she most enjoys doing with John, Carol says, is "just being together . . . even if it's home, watching TV or something."

"Just being together" fulfills the needs of many adults for a secure attachment and gives them a sense of safety and acceptance, as well as a structure for everyday life. Bernard, a gay graduate student in his late 20s, describes how he and his partner, Lawrence, care for each other by "being there." He has been living with Lawrence for a year, and he describes the comfort he gets from a quiet evening together: "I could just be comfortable sitting there reading and he would be sitting here reading, and we would be pleased just to be there together."[46]

Working together to run a household or raise children or adapt to illness or other crises are other ways that many partners care for each other. Providing practical help and support during illness often becomes an important part of caring for couples, especially as they get older. Marion and Grace are a lesbian couple in their 50s who are living together after a conventional life of marriage and children. Marion had surgery for cancer recently and often doesn't feel well because of her chemotherapy. One way that Grace cares for Marion is that she insists on doing all the heavy housework, to conserve Marion's strength.

However, as with many couples, the most important way that Grace and Marion care for each other is through psychological, physical, and sexual intimacy. "The thing that is important is the togetherness of our heads and the side-by-sideness of our bodies, and the sex is just a side issue really," Grace says. And Marion says, "I can talk to her about anything and I've never been able to do that with another person in my whole life."[47] A heterosexual couple, Lisa and Albert, who have been married for three and a half years, also emphasize intimate communication and acceptance. Lisa says, "Right from the start I was myself. . . . We talked openly and got to know each other first. That to me was more important than anything."[48] Most women and men in couple relationships probably depend on some of these ways of caring: sexual and psychological intimacy, cooperating in running a household and dealing with illness and other crises, and "just being there."

Although men tend to deny their dependency on a stable personal relationship, evidence from many studies shows that men are more covertly dependent on marriage than women for their health and well-being. Men who lose their wives through death or divorce are more stressed and much more prone to suicide and early death than women who lose their husbands.[49] Despite the masculine ideal of independence and the emphasis on individualism in American culture, most people seem to need a caring personal relationship with a spouse, lover, or friend. Gender relations, however, cover up men's dependency on being cared for and also undermine the quality of caring in their relationships.

Gender, Male Domination, and Caring in Heterosexual Couples

Caring in heterosexual couples is often undermined by the traditional pattern of provider husband and caregiver wife. This division of responsibilities increases male domination, as we have discussed earlier in this chapter. Also, it often leads to wives giving husbands a great deal of care and getting little care in return.

We can see this pattern in upper middle class and upper class marriages, where couples often describe their marriages as egalitarian. In these couples, husbands tend to have higher status paid jobs than their wives. Women's unpaid family caregiving typically gets little respect in the outside world, so husbands' activities and contributions to the family are defined as more important by the family. As a result, his needs and desires take precedence over hers, which is a form of power. She devotes herself to caring for his needs and supporting his career. The "two-person career," in which husband and wife are both focused on his career, used to be common for professional men. Now that so many wives of professionals have their own careers, the two-person career is declining, but it still flourishes among the very wealthy.[50]

The marriages of many very wealthy people dramatically illustrate how the traditional pattern of providing husband and caregiving wife can result in male domination and very little caring for wives. The wives of very wealthy men usually do not work and usually do depend on their husbands to maintain their luxurious lifestyles. The family's life revolves around the needs and schedule of the husband and his work.

Holly Gleason, who interviewed wives of very successful corporate executives in Southern California, found that the wives work hard at caring for their husbands, running the household, and raising the children. Yet, the wives get little caring in return from their husbands, little support for their own needs and goals beyond their needs for material luxuries.[51] One woman, whose husband heads a large international corporation and is frequently absent on business trips, would like to start a small interior design business, but her husband objects. "He just can't stand me having problems, or things on my mind. He needs me to have a clear head so I can help him work things out. I know I have a nice lifestyle and all, so I can't complain, but I am bored"[52] Another woman, who is completing a degree at a nearby university, describes how she arranges her schoolwork around her husband's schedule. "My school cannot interfere with our life; if it does, I will have to quit. I have to get home in time to fix a nice dinner, and fix myself up. . . . I go to bed with him, but when he goes to sleep, I get up and study."[53] His needs and preferences carry much more weight than hers.

When wives of CEOs face a crisis, their husbands are often too busy to care for them. For example, Jane, a woman in her 40s, had to go through surgery alone because her husband, Jay, was closing a major business deal in Chicago. "I did it alone. It was very frightening, but it had to be done."[54] When Jane's father died, Jay flew in for the funeral, but he had to leave the same day for a business trip to another country. For these very wealthy couples, male breadwinning and female caring resulted in extreme male domination and little caring for wives.[55]

Gender also limits caring in affluent and nonaffluent heterosexual couples by creating conflicts over love and intimacy. The struggle between women who want more emotional closeness and communication and men who withhold it is a major source of conflict in marriages and other heterosexual relationships and shows how traditional gender expectations can undermine caring. Wives typically want more intimate conversation with their husbands about feelings and personal experiences, researchers and clinicians report. Men tend to value intimate conversations less and prefer to express closeness through sex. According to marriage counselor Pierre Mornell, a middle class client typically asks her male partner for more contact. The man "experiences her demands (for longer talks, or an honest expression of feelings, or spending more time with the kids or her) as MORE PRESSURE." So he withdraws. And both of them feel uncared for and hurt.[56]

Working class couples in San Francisco interviewed by Lillian Rubin experience similar conflicts. One husband said, "I swear, I don't know what she wants. She keeps saying we have to talk, and then when we do, it always turns out I'm saying the wrong thing. . . . So I get worried about it, and I don't say anything."[57] Husbands may seek intimacy through sex, but they also are unsuccessful. Both husband and wife feel that they are not receiving enough intimate care.

These gender differences in intimacy stem from gender differences in expectations, opportunities, and power throughout the life cycle—the same social patterns that channel women into mothering and caregiving and men into breadwinning that we discussed earlier in this chapter. Women learn to value intimacy and personal talk through their childhood training for motherhood and femininity. Girls are taught to be sensitive to the needs of others, and to express feelings of vulnerability, which are key ingredients to intimate conversations. Boys, in contrast, are trained to be dominant and hide their weaknesses. As adolescents, girls much more than boys are pressured to focus on love and marriage. In adulthood, women's inferior economic opportunities encourage them to focus on relationships more than work and to be more emotionally and financially dependent on their marriage than their husbands are. Thus women more than men want intimacy in their marriages, which often creates a great deal of marital conflict and undermines caring.

Women's employment resolves some of the problems of traditional marriages by giving wives more power and autonomy. However, women who work for pay face new problems because caregiving continues to be assigned mostly to women, and there are few supports for family caregiving from the community or social programs.

Conflicts Between Paid Work and Family Caring

Women who become employed typically continue to do most of the housework and child care. Thus getting a job brings new problems to women and to the minority of men who are heavily involved in family caring; they are overworked and have too little time and energy to provide good family care, do a good job at work, and take care of themselves.

The problem of balancing paid work and family work continues to be seen as a woman's issue, and women do most of the adjusting. Employed wives still do most of the work at home. When family members need more care, women adjust by sleeping less or shifting to part-time or lower paid and more flexible work.[58]

Married couples and single parents experience work-family conflicts very differently, as we have described. Part of the difference lies in the fact that single parents are much more likely to be poor. In 1997, 32 percent of all mother-child families had incomes below the poverty level, compared to 5 percent for married couple families.[59] Affluent two-career couples have the luxury of being able to afford high-quality day care, household help, safe neighborhoods, and good schools for their children. However, succeeding in their careers often demands that they work very long hours, especially during their prime child-rearing years.

A special section of *The Wall Street Journal* on "Work and Family" describes the time pressures for upper middle class two-career couples:

> The Drill is relentless. Up at 5:30 to shower and pack lunches before waking, dressing and feeding the kids; out the door by 6:30 to drop them at day care and school; on to the office . . . scheduling meetings along the way.[60]

The schedule for working class two-job couples can be even more demanding. Transportation will take more time, if the couple can afford only one car or if they live a long drive or bus ride from work. Babysitting arrangements with relatives and neighbors may be less predictable than the day care centers favored by the more affluent.

For single working mothers with low incomes, caring for children's safety and health and providing them with a decent education become primary work and family concerns. Because of their low wages, many of these mothers must live in dilapidated housing in unsafe neighborhoods with poor schools and cannot afford good health care. Providing basic physical care and education for their children is a daily struggle, in addition to the time pressures of more affluent employed parents. The number of poor, employed single mothers is growing now that new welfare laws are forcing mothers to take jobs (most of them with poverty-level wages).[61]

Family members who depend on receiving care—children, the sick, or the disabled—also suffer the consequences of too much adult time and energy going into paid jobs and not enough time, energy, or money for unpaid caregiving. In families in which both parents work, children get less parental care than in traditional housewife-provider families because employed mothers have less time for child care, and most fathers do not increase their caregiving enough to make up the difference. Employed mothers devote an average of 6.6 hours a week to undivided child care, such as bathing, feeding, reading, and playing, compared to 12.9 hours for nonemployed mothers. Fathers contribute about 2.5 hours, whether they are employed or not.[62] Because of the heavy demands of paid employment and the lack of publicly funded social services, many family members are not receiving adequate care at home.

Perhaps the conflicts between work and family care will lessen in future decades. There are some positive signs of change, such as employers offering family-friendly benefits like flextime. New laws that grant workers unpaid leaves to care for family members are helpful for affluent couples who can afford to lose the mother's wages, but these laws do not help most poorer parents.

Social policies in several European countries provide useful models for how social programs can reduce the conflict between employment and family caregiving, as we will describe in Chapter 5. Most industrialized countries provide paid leaves for parents, as Exhibit 3.3 shows. They also offer citizens subsidized day care and assistance for the care of ill and disabled family members. In Norway, for example, employed parents are entitled to a leave of absence of 42 weeks at 100 percent of their usual wages, a policy that favors the right to care for children over the demands of the workplace. Attached to this program is a "daddy's leave" that reserves four weeks of this leave for fathers only; if the father doesn't use them, these four weeks of paid leave are lost to the family. The daddy's leave, established to change the gendered division of caring work, is being used by almost 70 percent of the eligible fathers.[63]

If family caring is left to individual families, without much support from government programs or community organizations, then the conflicts between employment and caregiving will persist. Women will continue to be burdened with lower incomes, little leisure, and considerable stress because of their responsibilities for caregiving, and children and other care receivers will not receive the care they need. For many families, these conflicts and pressures will become worse because of the growing burden of caring for chronically ill and disabled family members.

EXHIBIT 3.3

Maternity Leave Schemes, 1990

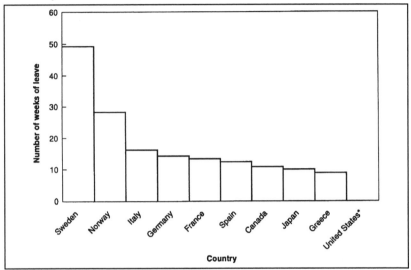

Source: Data used are from Gauthier,[64] p. 175.
* As of 1998, the United States still did not have a nationwide policy of compensation for maternity leave.

Family Care for People Who Are Chronically Ill or Severely Disabled

Caring for ill and disabled family members is another kind of caregiving that falls mostly on women. With the aging of the U.S. population and the shortening of hospital stays, the need for such care is rapidly growing. However, the economic and psychological burdens of providing it are substantial, and there is little assistance from outside the family to lighten the load.[65]

Recent Increases in Family Care for the Frail Elderly and the Chronically Ill

Contrary to the myth that Americans are increasingly abandoning older people to institutional care, families continue to provide most care for frail or disabled elders, except for financial support. Only 5 percent of all older people live in nursing homes, and the figure was only slightly lower in the 1950s.[66]

In fact, the amount of care that families provide for older adults is probably growing because Americans are living longer. People over 65 made up 12.5 percent of the population in 1990, compared to 8 percent in 1950. The population over 85—which is most likely to need a lot of care—is the fastest growing age group in the United States.[67]

Caring for family members who have acute or chronic illnesses is another area in which caregiving by families (mostly women) is probably growing. The expansion of hospitals since the 1940s took over part of the family's task of caring for the sick and dying. However, the availability of hospital care is now shrinking because of pressures to cut the costs of health care and reduce government programs. Increasingly, patients are sent home from hospitals quicker and sicker; family members are then expected to care for these critically ill patients at home.[68]

The Physical and Emotional Work of Caring for Chronically Ill or Disabled Family Members

What type of caring work is involved in helping parents or other relatives who are chronically ill or severely disabled? The work ranges from helping with transportation to complete 24-hour care. Researchers who study elder care often focus on the older person's need for assistance in *activities of daily living* (ADLs), which include eating, transferring from bed to chair, using the toilet, dressing, and bathing. They also examine the need for assistance with complex cognitive tasks, or *instrumental activities of daily living* (IADLs), such as preparing meals, handling money, taking medication, and using the telephone. About 15 percent of people age 65 or older need assistance with one ADL or IADL, according to U.S. Census estimates,[69] and most of these people are cared for by their families.

Severely ill or disabled older people often need a great deal of care over a long period of time. The best evidence comes from a large national survey of unpaid caregivers for older people who needed help with at least one ADL or IADL. Most caregivers had provided help for one to four years, and 20 percent had been caring for the disabled person for five years or more. Almost all caregivers provided assistance seven days a week and devoted an average of four hours a day to caring work.[70]

Most of the caregiving was done by women, the survey shows. Of the caregivers, 72 percent were women. Of all primary caregivers, 29 percent were adult daughters and 8 percent were sons. Turning to married couples, 23 percent of the caregivers were wives of the disabled person and 13 percent were husbands. Gender makes a very big difference in adult children's obligations to their parents; the obligation to care for an elderly, disabled spouse is more equal between husbands and wives.[71]

Caring for a very sick or disabled parent or spouse is not just a series of chores, as some studies of ADLs and IADLs suggest. For many family caregivers, it also means preserving the person's dignity and protecting the relationship between the caregiver and care receiver.

Preserving the self-respect of parents who are severely mentally impaired was a major concern of the middle class daughters interviewed by Emily Abel. One woman described how she creates pretend-chores for her mother, so her mother can feel competent. "I have accumulated things she can do so she feels useful. For example, I may just leave a pile of laundry totally unfolded, because that's something she can do and do easily."[72] Many daughters conceal their parents' dementia and pretend that their parents still have their old identity. Failure to provide this kind of emotional care is a major problem in paid, institutional care, as we will see in the next chapter.

The Costs of Family Care for Chronically Ill or Disabled Family Members

The physical work of caring can be a major burden of caring for disabled or ill family members. Many caregivers say that the kind of outside assistance they need the most is access to paid substitute caregivers who could give the family some relief from the endless work of caring.[73]

The mother of a 15-year-old quadriplegic spastic boy describes her day:

> First of all, in the morning, Michael's got to be got up and dressed and fed and toileted, and you know he's got to be held on the toilet—you can't leave him. It's a couple of hours really. And you can't do anything else while you're feeding him. If you turn round, it's spat out. It's a couple of hours getting him ready for school. And then when he comes home at half past three, your time is devoted to him. Someone has to be there. And when he goes to bed, you're constantly turning him. He has to be turned so many times before he goes to sleep. And he can be sick three times in the night.[74]

The stress of the physical work of caring may change over the caregiver's life span. The time demands of the work may be most difficult for younger caregivers who must add the work of caregiving to raising children or having a job. The physical exertion may be most difficult for older caregivers who are in poor health or are too frail to do heavy physical labor. In the national survey, the average age of caregivers was 65, and 42 percent of caregivers were in fair or poor health.

More affluent families often pay someone to do much of the physical work. For them, the greatest burdens of caregiving are the emotional strains of interacting with parents who are becoming increasingly disabled. They often feel responsible for preserving their parents' identity and health but usually are powerless to do so. However, caregivers in all social classes report high levels of psychological stress.[75]

Social isolation is another major burden for caregivers. Sixty-seven percent of spouses who cared for their elderly disabled spouse had fewer than four social contacts with others in an average week, according to a University of Washington study.[76] Caregiving for the ill or disabled also creates financial burdens because it interferes with the caregiver's employment, just like caring for healthy young children, and can create staggering medical bills for caregivers who lack medical insurance or access to government-supported health care. The costs of providing good care for ill and disabled family members are often too high for family caregivers to manage without outside help, contrary to the ideal of self-sufficient families. People who are ill or disabled may also need special care that the family cannot provide.

The Limits of the Self-Sufficient Family: Community and Government Support for Elder Care

The aging of the U.S. population does not need to be seen as a crisis. More Americans living longer lives is a good thing. Caring for the minority of elderly people who have major disabilities can be managed by most families, if adequate social services are provided by community groups, government, or private sources. Eighty-five percent of people over 65 have no major disabilities.[77] Most older people can continue to live independently with the support of programs like "Meals on Wheels" and home help who assist with housework, personal hygiene, and medical procedures. For family caregivers who take care of a chronically ill or disabled relative in their home, support services provide an important respite from the isolation and daily grind of caring. They make it possible to rest, get out, and see friends.

Many caregivers emphasize their need for services that temporarily replace the caregiver, such as transportation, personal care services, and adult day care, although others avoid using available services because of the stigma of taking charity or because of a commitment to doing it all themselves. Day care centers for older adults may take care of a disabled person during part or all of a day, several days a week, and provide social contacts, hairdressing, and educational opportunities as well as a meal and a bath. But existing centers in the United States are usually expensive, and they are unsubsidized by Medicare. A small but extremely popular program in England provides nonmedically qualified people, 24 hours a day, free of charge, who will replace the caregiver for a few hours when she wants to go out. The attendants will do everything from peeling potatoes to helping someone get on the toilet, and they are paid by a combination of government and private funds. Such programs are rare in the United States, so families, especially women, must struggle with a growing burden of caregiving.[78]

The potential crisis in elder care highlights the issue of responsibility for caring. Are men responsible as well as women? Is the wider community responsible as well as families? As their numbers grow, who will care for severely disabled older adults who need many services?

Conclusion

Families do most of the caregiving for children, for the ill and disabled, and for healthy adults living in families. Most of this caring work is done by women. Women and not men are channeled into caregiving by cultural beliefs about maternal instincts, by childhood socialization, by the job opportunities for women and men, and by men's power in marriage. Despite the fact that most American women are now employed, women in families are still expected to provide most of the hands-on care without much help from men. Families are still expected to be self-sufficient and care for their own members without much help from the community or government services. The economic and psychological costs of caregiving, borne mainly by women, are a major cause of gender inequality.

The reality of family caregiving does not fit the image of self-sufficient nuclear families, even in apparently "traditional" and economically secure families, like the Blaines, who depend on help from their relatives. The growing number of single-parent and poor families deviate even more from the nuclear image and need more outside assistance to provide good care. We will now consider some sources of care outside the family: paid care, care supported by government programs, and care provided by community organizations.

CHAPTER 4

Paid Caregiving

John Hopkins, a single man in his late 40s, has moved into the home of his old college friend Stephanie Dupin. She is dying of liver cancer, and he will be taking care of her at night. He is part of a close network of friends who care for Stephanie, and each other, "like a family." John and his friends believe that they can take much better care of Stephanie than a hospital or hospice. "The whole idea of being cared for by strangers for money. . . . That's not what I want for me or the people I love."[1]

Sometimes, paid care is the only kind available. And sometimes nurses, social workers, or other paid caregivers can respond to a person's needs better than their own families, contrary to the ideology of separate spheres. Catherine is a disabled woman who needs help with the tasks of daily living such as dressing herself and bathing. She values getting help from paid workers, as well as from Robert, the man she lives with:

> It's very difficult to ask somebody that you're also in a loving relationship with, it's very difficult to constantly ask them for the basic things you need. I find it's a sort of breath of fresh air in a way when my [paid] helper comes in and I have loads and loads of different things that I couldn't ask Robert to do.

Sometimes she might ask Robert to do those things, but with the helper "there'll be no strings, no other strings attached to asking, it's just a straight, can you do that."[2]

Paid employees are doing an increasing amount of caregiving in the United States. With the rise in women joining the labor force, in single parent families, and in people living alone, a growing proportion of American children and adults are being cared for by paid workers.

The quality of paid care, like family care, ranges from very good to very bad. This chapter examines the weaknesses and strengths of caring work in nursing homes, hospitals, social service agencies and other settings. We consider how the organization of caring work affects caregivers and care receivers, focusing on three features of paid caregiving: (a) the devaluation of caring work; (b) the impacts of competitive cost cutting and bureaucracy; and (c) the relative power of caregivers, care receivers, administrators, and outside experts.

Obstacles to Good Paid Care: Devaluing Caring, Profit-Making, Bureaucracy, and Hierarchy

Paid caring work has long been devalued, as we described in Chapter 2. Many of the concrete activities that go into caregiving are discounted. For example, nurses' aides who take extra time to comfort a distraught patient may be reprimanded because it takes them away from their scheduled duties of distributing medicines, cleaning and feeding patients, and filling out charts. The understanding and comfort they provide are not recognized as essential and skilled work. Also, the pay and working conditions for hands-on caregiving jobs tend to be very low. For example, nurses' aides and child care workers are paid less, on the average, than janitors.[3]

This devaluation of caring is part of a larger pattern of paying lower wages to women and devaluing activities seen as women's work. Women of color and immigrants, who are overrepresented in the lowest paid caregiving jobs, pay the greatest penalty, receiving the lowest wages and poorest working conditions in paid caregiving.

Profit making and bureaucracy add to the problems of paid caregivers. For example, health maintenance organizations (HMOs) have recently been charged with providing substandard care so they can increase profits. HMOs have cut down on staff, thereby increasing the work pressure on caregivers, and have reduced the length of hospital stays and other services. Government regulations and bureaucratic rules can limit the negative effects of cost-cutting by enforcing a minimum standard of care. Thus, several state governments have passed laws requiring HMOs to provide a minimum of one or two days in the hospital to mothers after the birth of a child and have set other limits on cost cutting.[4]

Bureaucratic regulations intended to improve care can backfire, though. For example, some state boards of health typically require that in nursing homes, a "Restraint and Position" sheet must be filled out for each resident every two hours of the 24-hour day (the sheet records residents' physical position and whether restraints are used to restrict their movement). This rule is useful for regulating the use of restraints to immobilize agitated or demented residents. It is also useful for bedridden residents, who must be turned regularly to help avoid bedsores. But for the other residents, the procedure has little value, and it keeps the staff busy with paperwork instead of providing direct care.[5]

Beliefs about separate spheres and self-sufficient families intensify the negative impact of capitalism and bureaucracy on caregiving. They encourage people to have low expectations of paid caregiving and to accept uncaring business practices and the unrestricted pursuit of profits. According to the ideology of separate spheres, caregiving belongs to the private sphere of the family, as we have discussed. The public sphere of work is expected to be impersonal and competitive, focused on making money and getting the job done efficiently. This expectation leads to the belief that people should not expect personal caregiving from paid employees, nor should they expect businesses to sacrifice profits to provide better care.

Beliefs in self-sufficient nuclear families and individualism imply that caregiving is the responsibility of individuals or families. It is not a collective responsibility among citizens. Americans tend to be individualistic and to reject the idea that they and their government have a collective responsibility to provide adequate care for all citizens. Compared to citizens in other industrialized countries, Americans give little support to restrictions on profit making that protect workers and clients, and they resist paying higher taxes to support government-subsidized day care centers, facilities for the disabled elderly, and other forms of paid care.

The third feature of caring work that we will explore is the distribution of authority and control in paid caregiving. In a nursing home, for example, how much authority should a nurses' aide have in deciding on an elderly resident's meals and snacks? How much power should be reserved for the resident or for the supervisors or medical experts? Many of the deficiencies in paid caregiving stem from unequal power relations and rigid rules that give too little power to hands-on caregivers and care receivers.

To challenge the assumption that only families can provide good care, this chapter first presents some brief examples of paid care that is "good": care that, in our judgment, seems adequate in meeting the physical and emotional needs of care receivers and providing decent working conditions for caregivers. Then we examine caregiving by nurses' aides in nursing homes, emphasizing the negative aspects of paid caregiving, especially the lack of emotional caring. We analyze the effects of profit making and cost cutting, the control over caring by bureaucratic rules and medical experts, and the devaluation of caring.

Then we consider some positive cases of paid caring in more detail to show how large-scale organizations can provide good paid care. We describe two workplaces in which caregivers have succeeded in raising the value of emotional care and have improved some of their working conditions and obtained more power over their caring work. We conclude by considering the power and autonomy of care receivers.

Paid Care Can Be Good Care

Under some conditions, paid caregivers can provide very good care. Day care can be as good or better for children than family care for some aspects of child development, according to extensive research that compares the development of children raised at home with those raised in different kinds of day care.[6] For example, compared to children raised at home, children in good day care centers are more intellectually developed. Good day care centers have caregivers who are better paid and better trained than the average, and they have a lower turnover rate. Their caregivers are responsive to the children and actively teach and play with them. The ratio of caregivers to children is high (about one caregiver for every three infants and one for every four toddlers).[7] The quality of care is usually lower in centers run for profit, because labor costs are kept down by hiring fewer caregivers per child and by paying them less.

Good paid child care is very expensive because it requires knowledgeable, mature, and highly motivated workers, as well as good wages to attract and keep such workers. Only the affluent can afford the best child care, unless it is subsidized by community organizations, business, or government. Good paid care requires acknowledging the importance of caring, providing adequate numbers of trained workers and financial resources for care, and making the care accessible to those who need it.[8]

Sioux Falls, a town of 100,000 in South Dakota, shows us how communities can provide good paid care by bridging the supposedly separate spheres of home and workplace. Companies and state agencies in Sioux Falls have agreed to assume some responsibility for caring for children and to cooperate with families. They reject the assumption that caregiving is the sole responsibility of women in families.

Sioux Falls placed first in a national ranking of the best places for mothers to work because of the excellent care available for children. Employers, city agencies, and community volunteers cooperate to provide child care and to support parental care. Citibank, the largest employer in Sioux Falls, subsidizes a day care center for its employees near its office building. In the wider community, the United Way spends 20% of its funds on day care, more than twice the average for the United Way in other U.S. cities. The school district has launched a privately funded after-school care program for 600 children, with reduced fees for low-income parents.

In addition to providing money and programs for child care, employers give workers time off to care for their families. Sioux Falls businesses employ a large labor force of low and moderately paid women workers who are attracted by family benefits. Thus employers have an economic incentive to provide family benefits, such as affordable on-site day care and flexible work schedules, instead of higher pay. In this situation, managers have come to value family caregiving as well as profits.

Supportive managers and community services help parents in many ways. Karla Quarve, a 31-year-old mother of a son in day care and a daughter in first grade, works as an auditor at a Sioux Falls bank. Her boss gives her time off for her family responsibilities, so she regularly helps out at her daughter's school and goes on field trips with her son's day care class. Community services are scheduled to accommodate working parents: Schools have switched parent-teacher conference times to the evenings, and physicians see patients after the standard work day.

Employers, government and community agencies, and families share responsibility for child care in Sioux Falls. "We don't take the place of parents; no one could do that," said Dennis Barnett, president of Sioux Falls' Volunteers of America, an organization that runs three day care centers in the city. "But we are partners with parents."[9]

Sioux Falls is an exception. Nationwide, very few employers offer on-site or subsidized day care, although a few firms such as Stride Rite and Campbell's Soup offer workers child care at or near the workplace, and some employers offer unpaid leaves to care for elderly relatives.[10] With a few exceptions, the U.S. business world and government remain unusually harsh and unsupportive of paid care or family caring, compared to other wealthy countries. There are relatively few restrictions on profit making that would protect families and little support for government regulations. For example, among industrialized countries, the United States is one of the few without government income supplements for parents of infants.[11]

As a result of these policies of business and government, and the overall devaluation of caring, good paid care is unavailable to many people. Paid caregivers struggle to do a good job despite low pay, poor working conditions, and little social support.

We will now look at caregiving in nursing homes, to show how good emotional and physical care can be undermined by profit making, control by bureaucrats and outside experts, and the devaluation of caring.

Undermining the Quality of Paid Care: The Example of Nursing Homes

Nurses' Aides: No Time to Care

Sara Wostein, an 85-year-old resident of a nursing home, is awake in the middle of the night. She is mentally alert, but very disabled physically. The nursing assistant or aide, Tim Diamond, one of the few men in this job, is checking each room. "Is there anything I can do for you, Sara?" he asks. "Yes," she responds, propping herself up and looking straight into his eyes, "stay with me."[12]

But Tim doesn't have time to stay. On the night shift he is responsible for 30 people and is busy checking each room and entering his room checks on the medical charts, sorting laundry, getting people water, and doing other tasks. Management avoids hiring more nurses' aides, to keep labor costs down and profits up, and state regulations demand that a lot of time be devoted to filling out charts.

Tim Diamond is a sociologist who took the training course and became a nurses' aide in Illinois. He worked in three different homes and studied them as a participant observer.

Tim's day as a nurses' aide begins with "punching in" at 7:00 a.m. On a typical day's shift, 63 residents will be cared for by four or five workers: three nurses' aides, one registered nurse, and possibly a licensed practical nurse or social service worker. Nurses' aides, who make up about three quarters of all health care workers in nursing homes nationwide, do almost all the hands-on caring for the residents.

Nurses function mostly as supervisors of aides. As Tim Diamond's instructor told him in his training course, "Registered nurses do the paperwork nowadays."[13] Nursing homes are also a world of women: Residents are mostly White women, and caregivers are mostly women of color.

A nurses' aide starts out by waking and dressing 15 to 20 people and bringing them to the day room for breakfast by 8:00 a.m. The residents are hungry. They haven't eaten since dinner ended at 6:00 p.m., and no snacks are available. After the meal has ended and the aides have fed those who cannot feed themselves, the aides have to record the nutritional value of the meal on each person's chart. This is required to meet the state's certification rules about nutrition.

During the day, it is hard for aides to find time to respond to people's individual needs. The residents are generally frail, physically disabled, and dependent on great amounts of assistance. Many of them are unable to walk and are severely mentally disabled. Thus the aides are kept busy feeding and cleaning people, giving showers, keeping records, and doing laundry and housekeeping. Because nurses' aides do not have time to supervise individuals, many people are kept in "restraining vests" that tie them to their chairs. Because there is no time to take them to the toilet when they need to go, residents are diapered.[14]

The small number of nurses' aides in relation to the number of residents creates intense work pressures. For example, in one home there were usually 30 to 40 people in the day room, many of them agitated, confused, or needing communication and empathy. The rule was that only one aide had to be present to supervise them, but other tasks like sorting laundry often called that aide away. "Usually, just as soon as we left the day room for an instant," Tim Diamond reports, "we had to rush back" because someone had wriggled out of her restraining vest.[15] The work pressures create a great deal of stress on aides and undermine the physical and emotional care that aides can give to residents.

Profits From Caring

The practices of corporate capitalism are responsible for much of this work pressure and the resulting poor quality of care. Nursing homes are a profitable industry in the United States. Tim Diamond describes an article in *Forbes* magazine that recommended investment in this growing industry in the early 1980s. Elder care is equated with generating profits, Diamond points out. The article advised that "the graying of America is a guaranteed opportunity for someone. How the nursing home industry can exploit it is the real question."[16] The title of the article, "Gray Gold," provided the title for Tim Diamond's book.

Under capitalism, personal profit is acquired through investing capital and employing workers, and the means of production are privately owned. Capitalism is grounded in the concept of free enterprise, or the pursuit of profit with minimal government intervention. However, good care requires considerable labor time. Paying for labor is one of the major costs in running a nursing home, like many other service businesses, so owners must keep labor costs as low as possible if they want to maximize profits. To reduce labor costs, for-profit homes hire a minimal number of nurses' aides and constantly change aides' work shifts to keep up a minimal work force. Aides are pressured to do all their assigned tasks on schedule, and those who deviate from the schedule are punished.

Wages are kept as low as possible. Nurses' aides started out at the minimum wage when Diamond was an aide, and they received tiny raises of 15 or 25 cents an hour. To make ends meet, many aides had two jobs, and they often moved to another nursing home in search of slightly better wages and working conditions. As a result of these low wages, there is a high turnover rate of nurses' aides, which undercuts the possibility of establishing caring relationships between aides and residents. The low wages also make it impossible for many aides to give adequate care to their own families.

The drive to maximize profits and cut costs has dramatic effects on the entire health care industry and social services, as well as nursing homes. The quality of care probably suffers in most cases. Understaffing results in intense work pressure, not enough time to care, and "burnout" by caregivers. Low pay and poor working conditions result in high turnover, which disrupts caring relationships and weakens the commitments of caregivers to their work.[17]

Recent changes in health care illustrate the effects of cutting costs on caregiving. Maximizing profits and cutting costs have become much more important in the health care industry, with the growth of for-profit hospitals, the massive shift to HMOs or managed care, and a new emphasis on reducing costs in government programs. All these changes give health care organizations, even those that are nonprofit, powerful incentives to cut costs.

Hospitals are laying off thousands of health care workers to cut costs, and nurses' workloads are growing. Kit Costello, President of the 25,000-member California Nurses Association, describes the reactions of nurses. "What our members are saying, on a daily basis, is 'I just can't keep up anymore,' " she reports. Nurses are being fired and replaced by nurses' assistants whose training often lasts for only two weeks. "As a way of cutting costs, hospitals replace nurses with less skilled people," reports a Chicago-based placement firm for nurses. "Inevitably there is a decline in quality."[18]

Sometimes efforts to raise profits and cut costs do not lower the quality of care. A report from the National Commission on Nursing describes an innovative program of nursing care at Carondelet St. Mary's Hospital in Tucson, Arizona that cut costs by focusing on preventive care instead of reducing labor costs and the standard of caregiving. Nursing care in this program focuses on the "nurse case manager," who "functions as a health care expert and advocate, seeing that patients get the care they need at the time they need it."[19] The case manager coordinates hospital care, home care, and other services, contacting the patient every month or every day, depending on the case. A two-year study showed that using case managers both reduced costs and improved the quality of care. Patients without case managers were sicker when they were admitted to the hospital and stayed longer. Two years of nurse case management saved the hospital about $1,550 per patient because of shorter hospital stays. Sometimes, quality care can be combined with substantial profits and cost cutting.[20]

More frequently, though, costs are cut by reducing the number of workers as well as workers' training level and wages, thereby reducing the quality of care. Thus, in the nursing homes that Tim Diamond studied, there were so few nurses' aides that they did not have time for emotional care. If nursing home owners and managers were not limited by state and federal laws, many of them would probably hire even fewer aides.

The push for profits can be limited by government regulations, pressure from unions and consumers, and a business culture that emphasizes serving the community and providing high-quality care. But even when profit taking is limited, other features of the modern workplace can undermine high quality care.

Control by Medical Experts and Bureaucrats

Caregiving in nursing homes and many sites of health care and social services is dominated by a medical model of care that reflects the worldview of doctors. Since the beginning of modern health care early in the twentieth century, caregiving standards have been controlled by doctors, as we showed in Chapter 2. This is still true at the close of the century.

In the medical model, good care requires hierarchical relations in which the doctors' orders are followed by nurses and patients. People's needs and problems are defined as individual pathology that requires treatment by medical experts. Caring, from this perspective, means scientific diagnosis, careful testing and charting, and treating parts of the body that are sick, not relating to a person's social and emotional experiences or the overall quality of his or her life.[21]

In nursing homes, state laws enforce medical standards because doctors are the most powerful lobby influencing policy in this area. A top priority of owners and administrators of homes is to meet state requirements so that the home will be certified and receive government funds. State requirements focus on medical care and the physical safety of residents and almost completely ignore emotional care. Administrators of nursing homes orient policies to satisfy state requirements, and complying with these policies takes up much of the working day of nurses' aides.[22]

The medical model of care and state regulations both ignore emotional care, so complying with these standards results in little time to care. After all the rules and regulations about medical care and patient safety are taken care of there is little time to provide emotional and social support or even to respond to the immediate physical needs of individuals. For example, in all three homes in which Diamond worked, vital signs—blood pressure, pulse, temperature, respiration—had to be taken and recorded for each person several times a day, even though many residents had the identical vital signs every day for years, as their charts showed.

Medical standards also shape values and rewards in nursing homes and hospitals. They define physical care and monitoring and charting medical information as most valuable. The emotional or interpersonal parts of care become secondary or invisible. Care in the form of talking to patients, holding their hands, validating their dignity and worth is not entered in the charts, required by management or state regulations, or rewarded by a raise.

The medical model improves the quality of care in many situations. If an elderly person who enjoys life has pneumonia or another acute, curable illness, most people would probably give top priority to obtaining expert medical care. Emotional care would be secondary.

The medical model is also strongly supported by the general public, especially in the treatment of acute, curable illness. Research on the attitudes of hospital patients and nurses shows that many hospital patients consistently rank expert medical competence as the most important aspect of nurses' caring. In one study, patients ranked these caring behaviors of nurses highest: getting patients their medication on time, starting and managing IVs properly, and knowing when to call the doctor. Hospital nurses themselves emphasized the emotional parts of caring and gave the highest ranking to listening to the patient, touching, and comforting. In contrast, patients in nursing homes say that emotional care is at least as important as physical care. According to one national survey, nursing home residents want caregivers that are "kind," "respectful," and take their complaints seriously.[23]

Emotional care is much more important in nursing homes than in hospitals that treat curable conditions, partly because most nursing home residents have incurable, chronic conditions. In addition, residents live in the homes rather than staying briefly, and they are very dependent on caregivers for their dignity and psychological well-being. For these reasons, many researchers, patients, and caregivers agree that providing emotional care and social support should receive higher priority in nursing home care.

Emotional caring also gets little attention in the formal training of nurses' aides, Tim Diamond reports. His training in Illinois focused on biology, anatomy, physiology, and nutrition, to prepare students for the certification test controlled by the State Board of Health. There was no training in how to clean a person who had defecated in bed, in a sensitive and efficient way that minimized embarrassment to the caregiver and care receiver. One exceptional instructor did emphasize the interpersonal aspects of caring. She taught students to practice "a certain kind of being there" with patients and to look into the eyes of dying patients and "to make that contact."[24] However, most of the training emphasized medical procedures.

Diamond learned the emotional side of caregiving informally on the job from an experienced and skilled nurses' aide. However, training by on-the-job apprenticeship to experienced caregivers is not formally recognized or rewarded. Including such apprenticeships in formal training would validate the knowledge of skilled caregivers, spread this knowledge to others, and raise the status of emotional caring. The current training system, dominated by the medical model, contributes to the invisibility and devaluation of emotional caregiving.

The "Iron Cage" of Bureaucracy

Bureaucracy also limits emotional and responsive care in nursing homes. Like the medical model, however, it has positive, as well as negative, impacts on the quality of care. Bureaucracies are controlled by impersonal rules and standards that are enforced by a hierarchy of officials. Ideally, bureaucratic rules lay out uniform procedures and schedules for carrying out tasks, regardless of who is performing the task, according to Max Weber, an early theorist of bureaucracies in modern society.[25]

Uniform procedures and a clear chain of command have many advantages in coordinating and directing large, complex organizations. For example, clear rules can safeguard fair treatment of clients and caregivers. Thus, in nursing homes, government regulations can protect residents by setting minimum standards for nutrition and the ratio of staff to residents and by preventing physical abuse through a system of reporting injuries and inspections.

Bureaucracy has serious drawbacks as a way of organizing caregiving because hierarchical power relations and standardized, rigid rules interfere with responding to the immediate needs of individuals. Such rules and relations undermine the autonomy of caregivers and care receivers.

The impact of bureaucratic regulations by government and administrators is vividly illustrated by caregiving in Crescent Nursing Home (the name of the nursing home, changed from the original, is that used by Nancy Foner). At Crescent Home, rigid rules and hierarchies, originally intended to protect the welfare of patients, became an "iron cage" (to use Max Weber's phrase) that blocked nurses and aides from providing high quality care.

Crescent Home is a 200-bed facility in New York City. It provides "above average" care, according to Nancy Foner, the anthropologist who worked there as a volunteer and researcher. Bureaucratic enforcement of medical standards may be unusually strong at Crescent Home because it is very large, and patients are sicker than the national average and older (the national median age is 81).[26]

In contrast to the homes that Tim Diamond studied, the main barrier to responsive, emotional care at Crescent Home seems to be bureaucracy, not capitalism. Crescent Home is nonprofit and unionized, and the nurses' aides receive good wages and benefits compared to other jobs available to people with little education. During 1988 to 1989, aides at Crescent Home earned $10.30 an hour; local child care workers averaged $5 to $6 an hour and garment workers earned about $7.50. As a result, turnover rates were low, averaging about 5 percent a year, compared to 40 percent to 75 percent in nursing homes nationwide.[27] Over half of the full-time aides had worked at Crescent Home for more than 15 years, and the ratio of aides to patients was substantially higher than in the homes in which Tim Diamond worked. Caregivers did not have to struggle with the low wages, high turnover, and intense work pressure of the for-profit nursing homes that Tim Diamond studied. However, they were under intense pressure from the hierarchy of nurses and administrators to comply with rigid rules and schedules.

In Crescent Home, too, there is little time for the emotional or social part of caring. "I never have enough time to sit and talk with patients, always rushing," comments one nurses' aide at Crescent Home. "I guess that's how they want it."[28] "They" are the administrators and the floor nurses who supervise hands-on caring by aides.

Caregiving at Crescent Home is controlled by federal and state regulations that must be met to obtain Medicare and Medicaid funds.[29] Government regulations dealing with nursing homes emphasize medical care and patient safety and ignore emotional care, as we have shown. They are enforced by state government officials who certify nursing homes and conduct annual inspections. In the state of New York, the inspections occur without warning, so homes must always have their paperwork ready for inspections. A top priority of the administrator at Crescent Home is to pass the inspection with flying colors. To accomplish this, he has strengthened nurses' control over nurses' aides.

The nurse coordinator on each floor, an R.N., is the most powerful person on the floor (except when administrators walk through). Her job is to enforce the policies of the administration and the government by ensuring that aides follow proper procedures. She writes the care plan that controls the daily work schedule of nurses' aides, such as when they take breaks or give baths. Any change in residents' food, medications, or physical positioning must be approved by her. The nurses' aides are constantly watched by the nurses, as the doors to patients' rooms are supposed to be open at all times.

For nurse coordinators, "their first priority is that regulations are followed," observes Nancy Foner.[30] "Good care," from their perspective, means that aides follow the care plans that they ordered. Thus, nurse coordinators believe that an aide who sits down to talk to a resident is loafing on the job; she should have plenty of time to talk while she is dressing or changing a resident and should not interrupt her scheduled routine.

The R.N.s, at the top of the nursing hierarchy, have a bureaucratic approach to care focused on complying with administrators and enforcing rules, not on responding to the needs of individual patients. The aides, at the bottom of the nursing hierarchy, are much more interested in caring for patients than in complying with rules. However, aides have little power. Those who try to provide responsive, emotional care have to fight the R.N.s who supervise them, and they often lose.

The Crescent Home bureaucracy defines the goals and tasks of caring in terms of state regulations concerning physical care. Could this bureaucracy organize more responsive emotional and physical care? If its administrators were accountable to broader, more humane standards of care that went beyond the medical model, perhaps bureaucracy would appear less an iron cage and more a way of organizing effective caregiving. Later in this chapter, we describe a model of nursing that tries to use bureaucracy to deliver humane care.

Race and Gender Inequality at Crescent Home

The hierarchy of control at Crescent Home reflects hierarchies of race, ethnicity, class, and gender in the wider society. At Crescent Home, the top administrators are mostly male, White, and well-educated. The nurses are all female, with one exception, and have diverse racial and ethnic backgrounds. All but two of the aides are female and all are Hispanic or Black, predominantly Jamaican. Aides' education level is low; about one third have fewer than 12 years of schooling. Like the wider society, affluent White men are at the top, and working class women of color are at the bottom. Unlike the wider society, however, the residents have the least power of all in many ways, although they come from the middle strata of society. The residents are mostly White women who were middle class.[31]

Racism creates major problems for aides and residents, the people at the bottom of the hierarchy. Some residents make abusive, racist comments to the aides, calling aides "nigger bitch" or "monkeys." "You say good morning to Mr. Buckley," a Jamaican aide said, "and he say 'Go away from me you black nigger.' "[32] These racist comments are hurtful to aides. In response they avoid close relations with residents, which can undermine the care the residents receive from aides. The bureaucratic control of R.N.s over aides also has a large negative impact on caregiving, however.

Conflicts Over Care in the Nursing Hierarchy

The negative effects of bureaucracy on caring are clearly illustrated by some of the coordinating nurses at Crescent Home. The R.N.s are primarily supervisors, not hands-on caregivers, but they have frequent contact with residents as the nurses monitor the work of aides. Most R.N.s consistently undermine emotional caregiving by aides, and they "are cool, often aloof with patients as they plow ahead with their paperwork and other official duties," Nancy Foner reports.[33] Only 3 of the 25 registered and practical nurses that Foner observed were gentle in their approach to residents.

In contrast to the nurses, most nurses' aides provide considerate and decent care to residents most of the time. Nancy Foner ranked about a third of the 35 regular aides on the day shift as excellent or very good in terms of kindness and sensitivity to patients, as well as in conscientiousness. She rated another third as good. Most aides talk to patients as they help them eat and adjust their feeding techniques to residents' needs. Aides also often have satisfying personal relations with patients, especially the more mentally alert patients who treat aides "like human beings" and ask them about their families.

Although Foner ranked two thirds of the aides as good or better, most aides were occasionally abusive or unkind. Physical abuse was rare at Crescent Home, probably because regulations against abuse were carefully enforced by state regulators, the administration, and the nurse coordinator. But emotional abuse was ignored; most aides occasionally yelled, swore, or insulted patients. Four of the 35 aides were usually mean and psychologically abusive.[34]

The contrast between the "best" and the "worst" aides on one floor shows how administrators and nurses value efficiency and following orders much more than responsive or emotional care. The nurse's favorite aide was Gloria James, an intelligent, energetic woman in her late 40s. Ms. James (as she was known) was efficient and neat and obeyed the nurse's care plan. Her rooms were immaculate. She had the beds made on schedule with decorated blankets (that she had provided) at the foot and items neatly stored in their proper location in the drawers. She worked fast, so she was usually the first aide in the day room at lunchtime preparing residents to eat. Her paperwork was done neatly and on time.

With patients, Ms. James was cruel and abusive, "truly frightening at times in her anger and vicious behavior" Nancy Foner reports.[35] She bullied and taunted patients to get them to eat on schedule.

> "I tell you EAT," she yelled at one woman in the day room. "You don't want to eat, you can die for all I care." When the woman meekly

complained that she could not eat because her foot hurt, Ms. James screamed, "Shut up and eat you. Eat. You think I have all day for you." And she turned to another woman, "You're such a nasty pig. You hear me, drink."[36]

Ms. James verbally abused patients in front of nurses, doctors, and administrators, yet she received the highest evaluations on the floor and was left in charge when the nurses were away. Efficiency and conformity to the rules were important, not compassionate care.

Ana Rivera was "the exact opposite" of Ms. James. The coordinating nurse judged her to be one of the worst aides and constantly criticized her. Ana, always called by her first name, a woman in her 40s, was warm, respectful, and emotionally involved with residents. Nancy Foner judged her to be "one of the best nurses' aides in the home and the one I would pick if I were a resident there."[37] But Ana irritated the coordinating nurse because she was relatively slow and often ignored bureaucratic rules and procedures.

In contrast to Ms. James' approach, at mealtimes she gently encouraged slow eaters to take their time. One lunchtime, as Ms. James yelled at residents, "Ana quietly fed a frail and weak resident, cradling her with one arm and gently calling her 'Mama' as she coaxed her to eat." When patients were abusive to aides and disruptive, Ana gently tried to calm them. One afternoon, one of her patients, Ms. Calhoun,

> went out of control, screaming and shaking when a new rehabilitation aide mistakenly put a restraint on her chair. Ana gently removed the restraint and stroked Ms. Calhoun's head for several minutes as she calmed her down.[38]

Ana's style of responsive care conflicted with rigid schedules and fixed rules. She was often the last one to leave the day room at lunchtime and failed to complete her paperwork on schedule. Sometimes she broke the rules and challenged the authority of the coordinating nurse to protect the welfare of her patients.

Ana caused a major blowup with the coordinating nurse when she ordered a new kind of glove to protect one of her favorite patients, a frail and partly comatose woman. After many requests from Ana, the nurse had failed to order the gloves, so Ana got them herself, in violation of the rule that any change in care must go through the nurse. The nurse was furious when she found out: "You cannot order things for the patient. You can only do what you see in the care plan or you will get in trouble."[39] The nurse never asked why new gloves were important.

She ordered that the new gloves be returned, and Ana did not bring up the glove issue again.

In this case, good physical care—protecting the hands of a patient—was probably jeopardized by the hierarchical, bureaucratic structure. Ana's style of caring—emphasizing responsiveness to the immediate, individual needs of residents for emotional and physical care—was ignored or punished by her superiors.

Bureaucracy has positive as well as negative consequences for caring. For example, Nancy Foner reports that in Crescent Home, physical abuse of residents was virtually absent, largely because supervisors carefully enforced state regulations about abuse. Uniform standards and procedures can safeguard the rights of care receivers and caregivers. However, residents at Crescent Home often received poor care because of rigid rules and the bureaucratic hierarchy.

Crescent Home and the homes studied by Tim Diamond show how caregiving can be undermined by unregulated capitalism, bureaucracy, and a solely medical model of care. We will now consider two other social patterns that lead to the devaluation of caring, the ideology of separate spheres and economic discrimination on the basis of gender and race or ethnicity. Then we will turn to positive examples that suggest how the quality of care and the working conditions of caregivers can be improved.

Separate, Gendered Spheres and the Devaluation of Caring

Why do capitalism and bureaucracy have such powerful negative effects on caregiving work? Part of the answer lies in the way modern organizations incorporated beliefs about separate, gendered spheres and the self-sufficient, breadwinner-housewife family. The dominant images of family life and the workplace became sharply separated in the nineteenth century, as we showed in Chapter 2. Caring belonged in women's sphere of the family, not in the workplace, according to the ideology of separate spheres. Caring was also redefined as a natural part of feminine feelings and not as productive work. The workplace, in contrast, was expected to be a heartless world of individualism and competition, focused on making profits and producing goods and services efficiently.

Separate spheres ideology devalues paid caregiving and justifies low wages for caregivers. Caregiving is seen as an emotional, natural activity of women that does not require specialized knowledge or training. "Real" work, in contrast, is defined as rational and impersonal (qualities associated with masculinity) and as requiring specialized knowledge or skills to advance. Insofar as caring is seen as unskilled and emotional, it does not deserve good wages.

The actual organization of work differs from this ideology in many ways. Obviously, caregiving is not confined to the family but is a very large proportion of the economy. For example, in 1990, the health care industry constituted over 12 percent of the gross national product and employed over nine million workers.[40] Even businesses that do not provide caregiving services often emphasize cooperation as well as competition and stress the importance of caring for consumers, clients, and coworkers. The belief that caring is a natural feminine activity that does not require specialized knowledge is obviously false for caregiving jobs that require a great deal of training, such as nursing or psychiatry. Nonetheless, the ideology of separate spheres is a key factor shaping the organization of caring work in the United States.

The ideology of separate, gendered spheres may also intensify the negative impact of bureaucracy on caring. Bureaucracies typically emphasize hierarchy, standardized procedures, and clear rules, all of which can be very effective in enforcing the values of the managers of the organization. When bureaucracy is combined with the ideology that the workplace should be rational and uncaring, then workers are systematically rewarded for efficiency, not for care. For example, an efficient and uncaring aide like Ms. James is seen as the best worker by administrators and head nurses because she best follows the administration's rational rules for patient care. In contrast, a bureaucracy that valued emotional caregiving in the workplace would reward workers who provided attentive emotional care; this possibility is illustrated by the Clinical Practice Model of nursing discussed later in this chapter.

The ideology of separate spheres continues to shape the choices and opportunities of women and men. Many more women than men are attracted to caregiving work because they have learned caregiving skills as they grew up and see caregiving as feminine work that confirms their identity as "real" women. Feminine identity is confirmed by being altruistic, emotionally sensitive, and concerned with the needs of others. Men, on the other hand, risk being defined as unmasculine, along with being underpaid, if they do caregiving work. Women, much more than men, are drawn to caregiving jobs not only because of their socialization and the expectations of others but because of their restricted opportunities in better paying, more prestigious and more powerful "men's jobs."[41]

Consistent with the belief that caring is part of women's natural essence, women college students often choose to be social workers, nurses, or teachers. They enter the helping professions so they can care for others. However, the same beliefs and practices that make caregiving appealing to women also devalue it as paid work. Caring work is undervalued and underpaid; therefore, women with better job opportunities often leave it.[42] Thus the lowest paid caregiving workers are drawn from the least educated and most exploitable groups: women of color and immigrants.

Caring Work: Underpaid and Undervalued

Many hands-on caregivers receive very low wages and little respect. Nurses' aides at many convalescent homes, such as the ones in which Tim Diamond worked, are paid close to the minimum wage.

Low pay for caregivers, who are mostly women, is part of a larger pattern of underpaying women workers and devaluing women's activities. In virtually all societies, no matter how their economies are organized, the work that women do is valued less than men's work. In the United States, jobs that are staffed mostly by women are usually lower paid than comparable jobs staffed mainly by men. Caring work is defined as women's work; thus it becomes a low-paid job.[43]

In well-paid caregiving jobs that are often held by men, such as family doctor or psychiatrist, men have successfully claimed authority as trained experts and have emphasized the scientific and technical aspects of their caring work to distinguish themselves from less-trained caregivers. Trained women professionals such as social workers and nurses have been less successful in securing recognition, authority, and higher salaries for their expertise at caregiving, as we showed in chapter 2.

For every dollar that a full-time woman worker gets, a working man gets $1.35. Women who are full-time, year-round workers in the United States earned 74 percent of what men earned in 1997. Although the pay gap is narrowing in the United States, women in many other countries do better. For example, in Denmark, Jordan, and New Zealand, women earn about 80% of men's wages.[44]

In a careful analysis of national data on the wages paid to different kinds of jobs, Paula England found that a major reason that women earn less than men is that women are concentrated in caregiving or nurturant jobs, and caring is paid less than other kinds of work. Her analysis

EXHIBIT 4.1

Wages of Caregiving and Other Service Occupations in 1996

Occupation	Average Hourly Wage (in dollars)
Cooks, fast food	5.74
Child care workers	**6.73**
Maids and housekeeping cleaners	6.84
Manicurists	7.40
Nursing aides, orderlies, and attendants	**7.75**
Janitors and cleaners	7.90
Psychiatric aides	**10.19**
Elevator operators	13.74
Flight attendants	17.52
Police detectives	19.84

Source: U.S. Bureau of Labor Statistics.[45]
Note: Caregiving occupations are shown in bold.

showed that "being in a job requiring nurturing carries a net wage penalty of between 24 cents/hour and $1.71/hour," regardless of the gender of the worker. The second factor explaining the pay gap by gender was the sex composition of an occupation. Predominantly female occupations are paid less. Paula England concludes that nurturant work receives low pay "because of its traditional link with women's work in the home and in labor markets."[46] Her analysis takes into account (or controls for) other factors such as workers' education, skill, and authority on the job. It provides clear evidence that the marketplace devalues both caring and women's work. The Exhibit 4.1 shows that service jobs that involve caregiving, such as "child care worker," are paid less than noncaregiving jobs such as "manicurist" or "elevator operator." Jobs that are typically filled by women, like "maid," are paid less than comparable men's jobs, like "janitor."

Racism also contributes to the low pay and prestige of caregiving work. African-American women earn about 65 percent of the wages of White men, and Hispanic American women earn about 55 percent.[47] Because many women of color do not have access to better paying jobs, they take caregiving jobs or other low-paying jobs, and employers who are motivated to increase profits and cut costs tend to hire them. As a result, both Tim Diamond and Nancy Foner report that most of the nurses' aides at the homes they studied were women of color, and many were recent immigrants. Once racial minorities and immigrants concentrate in low-paid caregiving work, racial and ethnic prejudices deepen the conviction that caregiving is low-skilled work. Thus inequality based on gender, race, and citizenship status all contribute to the low pay and respect received by caregivers.

Could hands-on caregiving be more respected and better paid within the framework of a modern, corporate economy? The evidence we have discussed so far paints a gloomy picture. We have seen how, in some workplaces, the pursuit of profits, bureaucracy, control by experts, and traditional ideologies of gender, work, and care all undermine the quality of paid caring and the working conditions of paid caregivers. However, other evidence suggests an optimistic view. In some workplaces, the organization of work encourages caring, and the value and quality of caring in most organizations could probably be improved if Americans enacted specific social changes, as we discuss in the final chapter.

We will now consider two particular workplaces in which caregivers have succeeded in establishing values and practices that encourage caring. At the first workplace, relatively low-status caregivers have established a more personal and responsive caring culture at the workplace in the midst of a cost-conscious bureaucratic organization. At the second workplace, nurses—relatively high-status caregivers—have challenged the system and tried to include caring within a modern bureaucracy.

Caregivers' Autonomy and Nonmedical Standards of Care: Case Studies of Good Paid Care

Women (and some men) enter caregiving jobs in part because they enjoy responding to the needs of others. At work, however, they are often blocked from attending to the needs of clients or patients because of cost-cutting policies, bureaucracy, and the other features of the workplace we have just discussed. Some caregivers respond to this frustrating situation by trying to change the workplace so that it supports caregiving. Caregivers with little status or power tend to avoid challenging their boss directly and individually. Doing so would probably fail and might get them fired. Collective action through a union would be more likely to succeed, but unions, up to now, have generally avoided the issue of giving greater value and pay to nurturant jobs.[48]

Instead, caregivers with little power use indirect strategies of resistance. In some cases, they develop an unofficial "work culture" with their coworkers that brings the caring values of the home into the workplace. Workers with little power often develop informal rules and understandings about their job in opposition to management, which social scientists have labeled "work culture." The psychiatric technicians that we will now describe were able to create a caring work culture based on family caring because they had greater autonomy from administrators than most hands-on caregivers and because their training emphasized emotional as well as physical care.

The Caring Culture of Psych Techs at Southern California Hospital

Psychiatric technicians (psych techs) caring for adults with severe mental retardation at Southern California Hospital illustrate one situation in which workers managed to provide better care and better working conditions for caregivers without changing the larger institution. These caregivers have developed values and practices in opposition to the administration's emphasis on balancing the budget and complying with government regulations. In many institutions for people with mental retardation, the work culture encourages a callous, disrespectful attitude to residents and defines caring as custodial. At Crescent Home, the work culture of the nurses' aides did not encourage emotional care. At Southern California Hospital, however, the work culture emphasized caring for each resident as a unique and valued human being and providing respectful and affectionate care.

Southern California Hospital and Developmental Center is a large state institution that cares for 1,100 severely retarded adults. Rebecka Inga Lundgren, a public health researcher, and Carole H. Browner, an anthropologist, studied the caring work of psych techs by working alongside psych techs and interviewing them.[49] Psych techs, 80% of whom are women, provide most of the hands-on care at Southern California Hospital.

The job of psychiatric technician in California was originally defined as unskilled custodial work and was filled mostly by men. There were no educational requirements. In the 1950s, administrative policy shifted to emphasize treatment and rehabilitation. In the 1970s, partly in response to pressure from patient advocacy groups, new policies emphasized the human rights of people with retardation to be cared for in the "least restrictive setting" possible. Psych techs became state licensed;

they were required to have a high school diploma and had to complete about a year's training in basic and psychiatric nursing.

Earlier studies of psych techs found them to be indifferent or even cruel to residents and uninterested in caring for the retarded, but the psych techs at Southern California Hospital "placed the highest priority on meeting residents' emotional and physical needs, and they resented anything that interfered with their ability to do so," Rebecka Lundgren and Carole Browner report.[50]

Many psych techs are emotionally attached to the residents and enjoy interacting with them and meeting their needs. Psych techs often touch and hold the residents. They initiate eye contact and interaction, even with the most severely retarded, and use their own money to buy room decorations, stuffed animals, and bedspreads for the residents. "I have fun here, actually, but I make it fun," a psych tech commented. "I come in, I greet my kids, I hug them and kiss them, you know. I play my music with them, I dance on the table top out there. I do. I bring them cake or candy or bake for the kids. Barbecue. I have fun. I try to make the best possible times I can." (Psych techs refer to residents as "kids," a sign of the family attitudes they bring to work and also of their tendency to infantilize residents.) Other psych techs get most satisfaction from helping their kids physically. "I've had a successful day when I've managed to get somebody's brace repaired or something," said one psych tech. "To me that's a great day."[51]

Some psych techs were attracted to their jobs for altruistic reasons. "This work is closer to the ideal that I had set up for myself when I was younger," one psych tech explained. "I went to a Catholic school and we were raised to desire a vocation—how you serve humanity and how you serve mankind. . . . I find coming in and trying to make someone's life more comfortable much more satisfying than other jobs I have had in the past."[52] But a caring work culture doesn't depend primarily on recruiting altruistic people. Coworkers train each other to be caring on the job, by teaching and reinforcing the values and practices of emotional caregiving.

The work culture developed by the psych techs reinforces a high standard of care. It includes informal rules that improve their caregiving and working conditions and encourage mutual support. For example, the psych techs encourage each other to evade administration policies that seem unreasonable or against the interests of the residents. They have developed a custom of being able to "walk" or leave the unit for a few minutes or hours when the stress becomes unbearable and they are unable to provide attentive care because they are about to lose self-control.

A psych tech described how she got help when she was about to lose control after a resident spit on her.

> I was so infuriated that I started to assault the resident. The supervisor saw what was happening and wrote out a requisition for a box of Kleenex. Then she handed the slip to me to go get it. . . . By the time I got back with the Kleenex, I had calmed down.[53]

The psych techs were able to develop a somewhat independent culture partly because they are not closely supervised. They have ample free time to socialize with each other when the residents are in school, and they have considerable power to decide how to interact with residents. In contrast, the nurses' aides at Crescent Home are closely watched by the nurses and have to follow a detailed Plan of Care. Psych techs have more autonomy than nurses' aides partly because they are licensed by the state (aides are not), so the supervisors of psych techs have less legal responsibility for controlling psych techs, compared to supervisors of aides.[54]

The psych techs were encouraged to create a work culture emphasizing emotional care, instead of just physical care, partly because of their training. The formal training and tests for psych techs are in psychiatric nursing, in contrast to nurses' aides, who are trained to follow the medical model of care. Also, because of the different physical needs of adults with retardation and residents of nursing homes, psych techs do not have to spend as much time on medical tasks as aides do.

The caring culture of the psych techs is limited by the hospital administration, which focuses on balancing the budget and complying with government regulations. Periodic budget crises result in hiring freezes that leave the psych techs short staffed. Then work pressure increases, and psych techs often lack the time to care for residents the way they would like to. Charting and other paperwork required by the administration or the state consume large amounts of time. Despite these limits, the psych techs are able to maintain a culture of caring. They are able to elevate their work from custodial services to caring with affection and respect. By doing so, they give their own work meaning and value, and they transform "the residents from social outcasts to human beings with special qualities of their own," as Lundgren and Browner observe.[55]

The quality of the psych techs' caregiving may also be limited by some of the negative features of family caring that are part of the psych tech's work culture, such as the tendency of parents to dominate their children and encourage their children's dependency. For example,

Lundgren and Browner report that the psych techs successfully opposed the administration's effort to reduce the psychotropic drugs given to residents, on the grounds that with fewer drugs, the psych techs would have to use harsher measures to manage the residents, such as physical restraints that would interfere with residents' social development. Although the psych techs believed their actions were for the good of the residents, perhaps the psych techs also were serving their own needs for playful, "caring" interaction with residents. Some of the problems associated with autonomous, paid caregivers are similar to problems that develop in families.

In this case, caregivers' training and supervision and client needs enabled caregivers to develop a relatively autonomous work culture of care, raise the quality of care for residents, and improve some of the working conditions for caregivers. However, because the workers lacked formal power, they could not address issues such as wages or the overall organization of the hospital.

Bureaucratizing Emotional Care: The Clinical Practice Model of Nursing

Higher status caregivers like nurses and social workers can sometimes draw on their professional status to challenge official values and practices directly. The Clinical Practice Model of nursing, developed by Bonnie Wesorick and used in several hospitals, directly challenges the medical model of care and the subordinate position of nurses in comparison to doctors. It gives nurses new authority to diagnose and treat social and emotional problems. It also uses central elements of the dominant work culture, such as record keeping and formal training, to increase the value of emotional caring and include care in the operating procedures of the organization.[56]

The Clinical Practice Model was developed in opposition to the dominant medical model, which defines nurses' caregiving as following doctors' orders and monitoring patients' physical condition and is aimed at curing illness and avoiding pain and death. In contrast, the Clinical Practice Model emphasizes nursing care that is independent of doctors and more holistic, although it also includes the traditional tasks of nursing. Nurses independently diagnose and help patients cope with their emotional and social concerns, as well as their physical problems.

The hospitals that adopted Wesorick's model changed the bureaucratic structure of nursing in several ways to support independent nursing. Nurses gained more power to diagnose and treat patients' needs, as well as time to carry out these functions. Nurses' training was redesigned to focus on the "art and science of caring" and to produce nurses who valued holistic care instead of the medical model.[57]

Wesorick developed a new system of charting patients that included the patient's personal history, religious values, family situation, and individual concerns. Attached to the standard chart focused on physiological information, this revised chart "became a daily visual reminder to all staff" of the importance of emotional care and the power and autonomy of nurses in providing such care. A new format for writing the Plan of Care was developed "documenting the patient's needs, concerns, problems, and describing personalized approaches to reach desired patient outcomes."[58] For example, a female patient was hospitalized with pneumonia. Her chart included not only physiological information, but additional notes to facilitate caring for the whole person: "dysfunctional grieving related to loss of husband two years ago, no support system, living alone, frequent use of Valium 'to treat feelings.' "[59] The Plan of Care included decreasing the use of valium and arranging for a volunteer companion and contact with the Widow Support Group.

This model adapts caring to the modern workplace by bureaucratizing and professionalizing care. Standard components of bureaucracy like formal training and charting are used to promote responsive and emotional care. To professionalize nurses' caring, caring is treated as highly skilled work based on specialized knowledge that requires advanced training. The knowledge in this case is the body of theory and research written by a network of nurses focused on caring.[60]

The Clinical Practice Model also gives nurses more power to diagnose and treat patients. On the basis of their greater authority and specialized knowledge about caring, nurses hope to be in a stronger position to claim higher status and pay, like therapists and other professional caregivers.

This strategy for encouraging care seems both very powerful and very problematic. It is likely to produce significant, long-term change, as it combines changing values and practices through redesigned training, with raising the authority of nurses, and using record keeping to enforce policies that promote caring. The Clinical Practice Model suggests that it may be possible to combine bureaucracy and care. Caring does not have to be treated as a natural emanation of a woman's personality. It can be redefined as a body of knowledge or set of skills and treatments that can be taught in schools, charted, and evaluated.

On the other hand, "bureaucratized care" may be a contradiction in terms. Responsive care, like the care Ana gives at Crescent Home, requires a personal relationship, a flexible response to an individual's unique needs, and an element of egalitarian "listening" to the wishes of the care receiver, instead of imposing authoritative "help." This kind of emotional care can be undercut by fitting it into predetermined categories and charts.

Professionalizing care is also risky because experts tend to dominate people. Experts, by definition, have specialized technical knowledge that is seen as very useful and is unavailable to most people. Therefore, expert caregivers often believe they should have the power to make decisions that affect care receivers, and care receivers often agree; after all, the experts are supposed to know what is best. By redefining emotional caring as expert knowledge controlled by powerful professionals, nurses run the risk of dominating patients and intruding on their personal lives. Changes that increase the authority and autonomy of care receivers might correct this imbalance.

Professionalizing emotional care may incur special risks of violating the rights of care receivers because emotional care involves close personal relationships in which the limits of appropriate interventions can easily become unclear. In the absence of systematic knowledge and universal standards of good emotional care, it is easy for caregivers to confuse caring for others with serving their own needs. Cases of psychotherapists sexually abusing their patients suggest that this risk is substantial. On the other hand, the benefits of therapy for many people shows that professional emotional care can be very effective.

For example, the widow described above might have a strong personal need or commitment to mourn her husband for a long period of time. She might feel that the nurse was being intrusive and manipulative in contacting the volunteer and the support group. The nurse certainly seemed to be judgmental in labeling her grief as "dysfunctional." Wesorick's description of the Clinical Practice Model shows no awareness that people from different cultures or religions might object to the nurses' values; it is also not clear that patients entering this hospital consented to receive emotional or psychological care. In some cases, the Clinical Practice Model might ignore the needs and desires of individuals as much as the medical model. It addresses the values of caregivers but does not seem to adequately consider the values and preferences of care receivers.

Should nurses or psychiatrists and therapists have the right to try to change patients' feelings and social support systems because they evaluate these feelings and behaviors as unhealthy? Answering this question raises complex issues of cultural diversity, patients' rights to control their own treatment, and caregivers' reponsibilities to provide "good" care. Strategies for improving caregiving need to strengthen the power of care receivers, as well as caregivers.[61]

The Care Receiver's Power

Attending to the needs and wishes of care receivers is the whole purpose of caregiving, so effective caring is difficult to provide without input from the care receiver. In some situations, getting input may be virtually impossible, such as in caring for a severely demented patient. However, even when it is fairly easy to consult care receivers, organizations that provide hands-on care or financial support for caregiving, such as hospitals or welfare offices, often fail to consult mentally competent clients about what they think they need. Control by experts, cost-cutting managers, and bureaucratic rules all operate against the empowerment of care receivers. Other trends, however, may promote the power of care receivers, such as the growing emphasis on pleasing the consumer.[62]

Some groups of care receivers who are respected and are politically organized have a great deal of power. For example, recipients of Social Security have had so much political power that for years, candidates for national elections have promised to do nothing to reduce Social Security benefits.

Care receivers with the least power, who are not politically organized, such as children or families on welfare, are rarely consulted about the care they need. People on welfare have virtually no voice in shaping welfare policies and are rarely even consulted. For example, in the lengthy Congressional hearings about changing welfare policies in the late 1980s, 246 people testified, only one of whom was a welfare recipient.[63] Because policies are created without understanding the life situation of welfare recipients, these policies are often ineffective or damaging, as we describe in the next chapter.

Some care receivers have increased their power in recent years by becoming more politically organized. For example, adults with physical or mental disabilities who are fully competent mentally but need assistance with daily living activities have organized for the goal of "independent living" for the disabled. Individuals and organizations representing disabled adults define independence as clients having control over the care and help they receive, not as doing everything for themselves.[64]

Jenny Morris, a researcher and advocate for disabled adults, interviewed 50 disabled adults in England from diverse backgrounds. She found that many disabled adults prefer independently paid helpers or helpers from social services to help from family members and partners because of the importance of independence to care receivers. One disabled woman commented that "for intimate personal care I prefer my sister or David to anybody else, but if it's for any other sort of care, I would prefer social services because I'm more in control, more directing things."[65]

Several disabled women especially valued helpers that they hired and paid for themselves, over helpers sent by social service agencies. The Family Aides sent by a government social service agency were described by one woman as "very patronizing" and "overbearing"; these helpers also were restricted by rigid rules.

In contrast, care receivers could control the helpers that they hired themselves. One disabled mother employed her own personal assistants (PAs) to help her function as a mother for her little daughter, Molly. With her PAs, she explained,

> I could tell them exactly what to do . . . you know, like if she [Molly] fell over and hurt herself then they were to pick her up and put her on my lap so it was me that did the kissing better. And of course Molly was fond of my PAs, but it was always clear that I was her mother.[66]

Another disabled woman employed helpers for assistance with her appearance. "It wasn't until I employed my own helpers that I could afford to think about what I looked like," she said. For special occasions, she needed someone to take a lot of time with her clothing and makeup. "They need to be patient and I'm paying for that patience so I feel OK about expecting it."[67]

Jenny Morris concludes from her study that paid caregivers often undermine the independence of disabled people because of "the assumption commonly held by professionals and care workers that they have the right to define what is needed and how help should be given."[68] For mentally competent adults, good care cannot be provided without granting care receivers considerable power to define their needs and control over the care they receive.

Conclusion

Paid care will become increasingly important in our society as the use of day care and nursing homes expands. However, the values and organization of many workplaces undermine caregiving, as we have shown in our analysis of nursing homes. Unrestrained profit making and cost cutting lead to too few staff with not enough pay, training, or time to provide responsive physical and emotional care. Workers who provide good, hands-on emotional and physical care are not rewarded with more pay, respect, or authority. The consequences for the quality of care and the well-being of workers can be disastrous. Good care depends heavily on highly motivated and well-trained workers who have time to provide responsive care. The lives of paid caregivers—most of them women and many of them people of color—depend on earning a living wage and decent benefits and working conditions.

Control of caregivers by medical experts, government regulations, and bureaucratic hierarchies can also block good paid care. Medical standards need to be balanced by standards for responsive and emotional care that meets the needs of care receivers. Regulations and supervision by experts and administrators needs to be balanced by sufficient autonomy for caregivers and care receivers.

Paid caregivers can be dedicated to the needs of their clients, like the psych techs at Southern California Hospital, or cruelly indifferent, like some of the nurses' aides at Crescent Hospital. The quality of family care also varies greatly. In both settings, good care requires committed, well-informed caregivers who have the time and autonomy, as well as the financial and social resources, that they need. Figuring out how to balance medical and emotional care or how to give caregivers and care receivers the autonomy and resources they need requires public debate about good caregiving. Resolving these issues requires new social policies to support caring. In the next two chapters, we examine how government and communities participate in defining and supporting caregiving.

CHAPTER 5

Governing Care

Americans give care as paid and unpaid caregivers. We also govern caregiving as citizens—through laws and policies and government programs. This chapter is about the ways government affects caregiving. In it are shown diverse forms in which citizens—acting through government—support, subsidize, regulate, and define caregiving.

Many Americans are uncomfortable with government supporting caregiving. They believe that individuals and families should be self-sufficient and that government involvement in caregiving is likely to undermine family care. Partly because of these beliefs, there is much less government support of caring in the United States than in most other industrialized countries.

In this chapter, we present a more detailed comparison of U.S. policies of caregiving and policies of other countries. We examine how current government policies and programs took shape in a gendered society and how they contribute to gender inequality. We also consider two puzzling questions about government and caregiving: First, does government enhance or undermine care? Second, can laws and policies expand caregiving without maintaining gender inequality?

How Do Governments Support Care?

Government Subsidies and Services

Anyone who has grown up in the United States since World War II knows many of the ways in which government supports care. Contrary to American ideals of individualism and self-sufficient families, caregiving in most families is shaped by government programs, policies, and laws. Elders, in particular, know the benefits of government-supported care. Social Security retirement benefits have enabled many elders to live independently and have permitted their children to devote family income to their children's care instead of care for dependent parents. Medicare health benefits, the only government health program available to everyone (once they are old), have improved the health of America's elders, particularly the large numbers who would have been uninsured or underinsured in their latter years. Medicaid health insurance for the poor has allowed elders who are ill and impoverished to receive additional subsidized care; for example, admission to nursing homes.

Since 1959, when over one third of the elderly lived in poverty, Social Security benefits and Medicare have greatly reduced poverty among elders: now only 12 percent live in poverty.[1] (The poverty rate is twice as high for elderly women than men, and we will soon see why.) Government programs for elder care have placed elders among the most economically secure Americans and won widespread citizen approval and support.

Children have also benefited from government care but not nearly so extensively as elders have. Government provides tax exemptions to families rearing children. Various levels of government support schools and colleges, parks and recreation. We intervene on behalf of children whose families abuse and neglect them. We outlaw children's economic exploitation. In general, though, our programs and policies have assumed that families protect and care for their own children with little direct public support. Most Americans believe they have little collective responsibility for the care of all children. This is how Americans thought of elder care before we developed old age programs in the 1930s. As a result, children are nearly twice as likely to live in poverty as elders and are more likely to be medically uninsured.[2]

In Europe, on the other hand, social security has extended to other age groups, as well as elders. Virtually every other developed country in the world insures its citizens' medical care, subsidizes parental leave for parents of young children, and provides supports for caregiving, like family allowances or child care services, to families rearing children, as well as subsidies for housing and other social services. In contrast to the United States, most European countries also give elderly women benefits as citizens that are not tied to husbands' benefits, so they are much less likely to be poor than elderly women in the United States. In most industrialized countries, these forms of government care are available to everyone, so people are proud of them the way most Americans are of Social Security, even though they may complain of high taxes. The most affluent European families "return" the benefits in higher income taxes. Families at risk of poverty, such as those headed by single mothers, are protected from impoverishment and from the stigma of being the only apparent beneficiaries of public care.[3]

Social programs and government subsidies are not the only way that government provides care. Education is often not recognized as a form of care, but one of the arguments for the expansion of public education in the United States early in the century was that schools could offer the supervision and teaching that families in an urban industrial economy could not always provide.[4] Contemporary debates over whether or not government should support child care raise issues about the needs of families for help in caregiving and the proper role of government that were first raised when the United States considered public education.

Regulating Care

In addition to providing subsidies and services of care, governments regulate the way other institutions affect care. The Family and Medical Leave Act of 1993 requires large employers to allow family members unpaid time off work to care for a new baby (European democracies all require and subsidize paid leave for parents of newborns; see Exhibits 3.3 and 5.1). State child care regulations limit the numbers of children that child care workers can care for at one time. Laws also limit the working day to eight hours, which protects parents' rights to have time for family caregiving.

Deciding Who Can Give and Receive Care

Laws and policies also determine who among us is entitled to care and from whom. Laws require parents to care for and supervise their children, defining parental rights and obligations to care. Laws regarding child abuse define the limits of parental violence and neglect in child rearing. Before child abuse laws existed, parents had a nearly unlimited right to neglect children or violently punish them.[5]

Divorce and child custody laws identify the caregiving obligations of each of the divorcing parents. For example, a child custody agreement might allow a father who has been a neglectful caregiver to visit his children but not to take care of them overnight. Even so, the mother who had left the workforce to care full-time for her children, and who will do all caregiving for them after the divorce, may be denied alimony because the court decides that she and the noncaregiving father are "equally" capable of self-support.

Marriage law defines who may become family to each other. Gays and lesbians (and at one time, biracial couples as well) may not legally marry. This leaves partners without the social support that legal marriage gives to a couple's commitment to care. It also leaves them without legally recognized family members' rights to use employee medical insurance or retirement benefits to care for each other. Family law also leaves gays or lesbians who have been caregiving, but not biological, parents without child custody rights if the biological parent dies or the couple separates; they may even be denied rights of visitation.[6]

Indirect Government Provision

We can think of hundreds of ways in which government directly defines, regulates, subsidizes, or provides care. In addition, law and policy also *indirectly* shape access to care. Various kinds of income tax deductions or credits indirectly help families provide care. Dependent child deductions are aimed directly at caregiving, for example, and mortgage interest deductions indirectly subsidize care in the form envisioned in the American Dream: the family home. The family-owned home is widely considered the ideal site of self-sufficient family care. Americans who can afford it usually become homeowners in the family caregiving stage of life and depend on paid-up mortgages to keep them independent in their old age. Mortgage interest deductions are an example of indirect government support for caregiving.

Indirect supports very often have an unrecognized element: government supports "target" the middle and upper classes. Low-income and working class people are less likely than others to receive their benefits.[7] In 1995, for example, tax breaks for homeowners cost the federal government $72.5 billion, more than three times the Aid to Families with Dependent Children (AFDC) budget. The richest 6 percent of taxpayers received half of all mortgage interest deductions; their tax breaks cost the federal government more than the entire budget of Housing and Urban Development (HUD), the federal agency that subsidizes housing for the poor.[8]

We rarely call government care benefits that disproportionally affect the affluent "welfare," but they are government provisions that parents use to better care for their children. "Welfare" provisions like these are vastly more expensive than the caregiving services for the poor we call welfare. Welfare for the poor is a direct subsidy that is easy to recognize and, as we have seen in recent years, easy for taxpayers to target for repeal.

Gender, Care, and Welfare
in the United States

The welfare system is the arena of government most people view as supporting caregiving. Although there is no official government organization with that name, the "welfare system" is the whole range of laws, policies, and programs that directly provide for those who are less able to provide for themselves—for example, those who are sick, disabled, unemployed, poor, aged, or children. It includes Social Security and unemployment insurance, as well as food stamps and programs to assist poor single mothers. This section describes how the United States' welfare system developed historically and how it influences gender inequality between men and women and between the affluent and the poor.

In the 1930s, following the long and harrowing Great Depression, Congress approved a massive federal system to protect citizens against destitution and the kinds of family and community breakdown that poverty, disability, and unemployment can foster. The array of safety net programs that took shape in President Roosevelt's New Deal, like old age and unemployment insurance and aid to poor children, became the basic "entitlements" of the U.S. welfare system. Since the 1930s, the U.S. national welfare system has added programs like food stamps, Medicare, and Medicaid. In 1996, Congress ended entitlement for the poor and shifted to limited support for state-run programs.[9]

Some countries define welfare more broadly—as programs for the welfare of *all* citizens. Welfare in these countries includes education, health, housing, and other universal benefits. Later on, we compare government-supported care in these countries with care in the United States. First, we focus on how our arrangements of government care were influenced by ideas about caregiving and gender and how they affect patterns of caregiving and gender inequality.

Two Tiers of Government Support

The Social Security Acts of 1935, which founded the core programs of our national welfare system, created two kinds of benefits for welfare recipients: social insurance and public assistance. Social scientists sometimes call these two kinds of programs "tiers" because programs in the social insurance tier are superior—that is, more generous and honorable—compared to programs of public assistance.[10]

The "top" tier, social insurance programs, provides benefits to people in all income groups who become eligible because of their employment history or events we think of as beyond their control: unemployment, old age, injury, or disability. Most of these programs were envisioned as insurance for stable employees or for retired workers and their dependent wives and children. No one needs to prove economic need to claim these benefits; they are the "rights" or "entitlement" of all productive citizens. We see them as "contributions" we make through taxes on our earnings. By far, most of our federal welfare dollars are spent on Social Security, Medicare, and other social insurance programs.[11]

The second tier, public assistance, includes programs, such as AFDC and food stamps, that we refer to as "welfare." These benefits are only available to those who can prove economic need. Recipients must account for their expenses and their living arrangements to become eligible. Because public assistance is only for the impoverished and needy, Americans tend to regard it as a form of charity.[12] Although most people who receive public assistance are caregivers (single mothers taking care of children), Americans usually do not think of this tier as a right or entitlement of caregivers. They think of public assistance as charity for the poor that is paid for by taxing productive citizens. Thus recipients of assistance are treated like "dependents" rather than like entitled citizens.

Contrary to popular belief, these two tracks of government provision are funded similarly. Authorities call Social Security a "contributory" or insurance program, implying that people receive benefits according to the amount they have contributed. This is a fiction used to give legitimacy to insurance programs and to stigmatize public assistance. Individuals do not draw Social Security from contributions they have paid into individual accounts. Both insurance and assistance programs are funded by pooled taxes. Most people who collect Social Security will collect far more than they paid in. Most people who collect welfare "contributed" at least some of it through their previous income taxes and through payroll and excise taxes (and these last two take a much bigger bite out of the earnings of the poor than the affluent).[13]

The two tiers of entitlement are not just unequally generous and honorable, they are also unequally gendered. Most social insurance benefits go to men and, through them, to women and children who are their dependents. Many employed women are ineligible for unemployment benefits, which require a male "breadwinner" pattern of uninterrupted work. In old age, they are likely to receive spousal benefits (a portion of their husband's retirement benefits) instead of the even lower ones they could claim as retired workers. The smallest and more stigmatizing public assistance benefits mostly go to women and the children who are their dependents.[14]

In sum, our two-tiered welfare system provides relatively generously to breadwinners, regardless of current income; ungenerously to impoverished caregivers; and nothing directly to caregivers who are not poor. Claiming benefits as a breadwinner is superior to claiming them as a needy caregiver. Receiving social insurance is businesslike and honorable. One enrolls and collects by mail. There is enormous popular support for social insurance programs, especially Social Security; opponents of the programs have never been successful politically.[15]

Receiving public assistance, on the other hand, is humiliating and dishonorable. Participants must be interviewed frequently by "case managers," repeatedly prove eligibility, and participate in counseling, rehabilitation, or other supervised activities. Means-tested welfare programs are unpopular and have always been politically vulnerable to attack.[16] One might expect a welfare system to reward those who provide unpaid care for children, the old, and the disabled. Ours, instead, rewards earners far more than carers.

Caregiving in the History of the U.S. Welfare System

The nineteenth-century gender ideology of "separate spheres," which so influenced the gendered division of labor in earning and caregiving, also influenced the ways we have organized government support for care. If we examine the origins of our system of social welfare provision, we can see the impact of gendered assumptions about earning and caring.

The history of the present system holds some surprises: Even before women were voting citizens, American women formed an organized political force that influenced the shape of our welfare system. They aimed to strengthen the social value of caregiving. Nonetheless, in the end, breadwinning became the activity that entitled a person to superior government care.

Mothers' Pensions in Recognition of Care

Our earliest systems of aid to the poor were primarily local—partly voluntary, partly government supervised. At the turn of the twentieth century, as massive immigration and urban growth proved the futility of purely local solutions to poverty, pressure mounted in favor of a national effort to ease the ravages of a capitalist economy. A national network of women active in local charity and moral reform organizations lobbied for a system of "mother's pensions."[17]

Mother's pensions were supposed to enable "worthy," poor widows (and some divorced women) to keep their children, rather than place them in orphanages, which is what single mothers often had to do. With aid to single mothers, caregivers would serve the public interest by caring for children in the home. The idea of pensions for those who served the nation existed in the form of pensions for Civil War veterans. Advocates of mothers' pensions wanted recognition that caregivers also serve the nation.

These networks of female reformers and charity workers—mostly White and middle class—carried widely shared ideals of separate spheres into early twentieth-century government programs. The women called themselves "public mothers" or "maternalists." Maternalists believed that women were naturally and uniquely gifted to be caring mothers and that domestic motherhood should be socially valued and supported. Maternalists also believed that domestic motherhood should be economically supported by breadwinner husbands. Only "deserving" mothers without breadwinners—honorable widows, not mothers who were single because of "immoral" choices of divorce or illegitimacy—should receive social pensions.

A network of middle class Black women shared the maternalism just described but, nonetheless, acknowledged that many poor women had to work for pay. As a result, they worked for day care for employed mothers, as well as mothers' pensions. Their vision of support for women's earning *and* caring was not influential at the time because racial minorities were excluded in most political coalitions, female as well as male. Black women's activism resulted in the formation of many community child care and health care institutions, but their vision of public supports for maternal employment as well as caregiving was not widely accepted until now.

By the mid-1920s, in response to the mobilization of local women's groups throughout the country, 46 of the 48 states adopted forms of mothers' pensions, most in the previous decade. The political success of the idea of government support for caregivers did not translate into expansive programs or generous benefits, however. Benefits were kept extremely low so as not to compete with marriage to a breadwinner. The programs also served few people; local business interests never wanted to undercut the supply of low-wage workers.

Many needy single mothers were denied pensions on moral grounds: if they were divorced or had children out of marriage or if they drank or were otherwise "unworthy." Few African-American mothers were included. In Los Angeles, women of Mexican background were excluded on the grounds that their inferiority made them too likely to abuse aid. At harvest time, Southern towns withdrew all forms of poor relief to women as well as men to assure themselves field workers. Nonetheless, the spread of mothers' pensions demonstrated popular support for government support of caregiving and recognition of the caring work of mothers.

The Children's Bureau: First National Government Agency for Caregiving

The same national network of maternalist women's organizations that worked for mothers' pensions lobbied and agitated until, in 1912, Congress established a Children's Bureau in the U.S. Department of Commerce and Labor and dedicated it to the welfare of children. Run entirely by women, the bureau framed its activities in close contact with local women's clubs, reform groups, charities, and social workers, and in personal correspondence with mothers from all regions and social classes. It conducted research on infant mortality, published pamphlets on infant and child health, and activated local support for mothers' pensions.

Mobilizing its national network, the Children's Bureau helped to pass the first national welfare bill, the Sheppard-Towner Maternity and Infant Protection Act, in 1922. The bill provided federal matching funds to states to set up prenatal and mother-infant health clinics and to subsidize public health nursing and instruction. The Sheppard-Towner Act was opposed by the medical profession because it was government-sponsored health care (perceived as threatening doctors' autonomy and economic interests). Still, they could not defeat the program for seven years. In the years it survived, with only modest funding, many millions of families received pamphlets on child health protection, millions were visited by health workers, and thousands of prenatal centers were built.

The New Deal: A Safety Net for the Working Man

Mothers' pensions and the Children's Bureau programs did not last long. The movement toward a national welfare program was soon dominated by concerns about protecting breadwinners, not caregivers. New political coalitions in the 1930s addressed the widespread unemployment and economic devastation caused by the Depression. These coalitions brought together business interests, which wanted to stabilize the volatile industrial economy, and labor interests, which wanted to protect stable male workers from unemployment.[18]

These groups pushed for policies that treated caregivers as beneficiaries of breadwinners rather than as people with an independent right to social services because of their unpaid caregiving work. Only breadwinners deserve citizens' benefits of government aid, they argued (although, at the time, they also excluded agricultural or seasonal workers, who were disproportionally minority men). They ignored the claims of citizenship based on caregiving that many maternalists advocated.

The Social Security Acts of 1935 laid the enduring foundation of the U.S. welfare state. This was the two-tiered system that we have just described in its current form. The centerpiece of the legislation was the top tier of old age and unemployment insurance. The influence of maternalist welfare activists was registered in the acts' provisions for impoverished nonearners, which we now call "welfare." Aid for Dependent Children (ADC), which eventually became Aid to Families with Dependent Children (AFDC), encouraged mothers to stay at home to care for children, rather than forcing them into employment. ADC (and, later, AFDC) also incorporated the stigmatizing "charity" patterns of mothers' pension laws: means testing, morals inspection, low benefit levels, and local control and discretion. Built into the foundations of the contemporary welfare system, the maternalist commitment to the breadwinner-caregiver ideal enabled widowed mothers to keep and care for their children rather than orphan them. The same commitment also favored a system in which dependence on a breadwinner was the *only* route to a mother's and children's economic well-being and dignified access to social provision.

The Breadwinner-Caregiver Ideal and the Welfare System

Separate spheres ideals elevated caregiving as a moral good, but these ideals also defined caregivers as the dependents of breadwinners and helped produce a welfare system in which only breadwinners were citizens worthy of dignified government care. Caregivers were second-class citizens who received only derivative benefits of citizenship rather than autonomous ones. Government care became gendered and unequal in ways that paralleled the gender inequality of the economy and the family.[19]

The emerging welfare system also gave unequal benefits to families. Breadwinner-caregiver families received the best treatment because they received benefits through social insurance programs, such as Social Security and Unemployment. Women in such families receive government benefits, even though indirectly, as dependents. Even early in the century, however, the breadwinner-caregiver ideal was hard to achieve. In many two-parent families, a breadwinner's low wages could not subsidize full-time caregiving. Yet government policy neither assured a family-supporting wage for male breadwinners nor provided caregiving supports, such as day care or paid parental leave, that would help mothers both earn and care.[20] Those who could not achieve the ideal, and those who considered the sharing of earning and caring a better family arrangement, would be slighted by the developing forms of government provision.

Building the breadwinner-caregiver ideal into the new system of government care *institutionalized* the ideal. Even now that most women are employed, and the breadwinner-caregiver division of labor is impractical or unappealing for a majority of families, the government programs we established long ago continue to reward and enshrine the breadwinner-caregiver ideal. They maintain gender inequity and stigmatize families that do not fit the ideal. Embedded in our law, policy, and programs, the breadwinner-caregiver ideal justifies the continuing assumption that workers are breadwinners who have no caregiving responsibilities. It justifies low wages for jobs dominated by women and low benefits to mothers rearing children alone. It also justifies husbands' delegation of caregiving to wives, even now that most wives are employed mothers.

When government provision does not recognize caregiving as productive labor that entitles a caregiver, independently, to the benefits of citizenship, it perpetuates mothers' economic dependence on marriage, whether or not the marriage is safe for the mother or children.[21] This kind of government support also perpetuates beliefs that women are natural caregivers and that care is a female way of being instead of every citizen's social obligation. By institutionalizing the breadwinner-caregiver ideal, our welfare system has perpetuated gender inequality.

The End of the Safety Net and the Disappearance of Debate on Care

Although early AFDC was created to support single mothers' caring work, there was always a tension between public expectations of breadwinning and caregiving for single mothers. Should they stay home and take care of their children or get a job and leave their children alone or in others' care? By the 1970s, worldwide economic changes had made government programs less popular. More of the poor entered the welfare system, making welfare more costly. Greater proportions of welfare claimants were divorced mothers or mothers who had never married, triggering public disapproval of support for the "unworthy" poor.[22] In addition, growing numbers of nonpoor mothers had entered the labor force, many of them under economic pressure. Increasingly, government support appeared to grant poor women a "luxury" other women could not afford: staying at home to care for children.

A series of federal policies to put poor single mothers to work began in the 1960s and grew in size and scope until, in 1996, Congress voted to end AFDC, the federal guarantee of a safety net under single mothers and their children. The new law gives states authority to decide on eligibility and benefits. It limits federal funding and sets upper (not lower) time limits on a family's eligibility for federal funds.[23]

We cannot report on the effects of the end of welfare because the law has only recently gone into effect. We do know that some states already plan to end support for caregiving altogether and use funds for workfare (mandatory work programs) rather than welfare. Wisconsin has already done this. Economists predict that job shortages and worker problems (such as illiteracy and addiction) will limit the employment of mothers on welfare and the reemployment of "working poor" mothers who are displaced by former welfare recipients.[24] However, as we go to press, a boom economy may be delaying these effects.

Congress's research agency predicted that a million more children will enter poverty. Child protection authorities worry that children whose mothers cannot support them will flood into the foster care system.[25] One day's newspaper accounts portray single mothers who quickly found jobs in the booming economy and who are proud to be self-supporting. The next day's coverage features less successful single mothers who have not found gainful work and who fear losing custody of their children for failing to provide for them.

A remarkable change in public dialogue took place in the decades of debate over welfare reform for single mothers. Over time, discussion of caregiving withered, and finally, it virtually disappeared altogether. In contrast to earlier "maternalist" concerns about children's needs for love, supervision, and guidance, by the 1990s, policy makers referred only to children's needs for "self-reliant families" and for mothers who modeled the "work ethic" in the absence of fathers.[26]

In the wider political arena, public concern about family-friendly policies—such as parental leaves and child care—that recognize workers' needs for time and help with caregiving had finally attracted public attention and congressional action. This made it all the more startling that welfare reform had ceased to be discussed as a work and family issue and that single-mother caregiving had become invisible.

Images of Caregiving in Policy

One way that poor, single mothers' caregiving work became invisible in policy debate was the repetition of the idea that single mothers should be "like other working mothers." This phrase, used repeatedly by politicians, journalists, and people on the street, conveyed an image of the modern family that was as distorted as it was persuasive. Its truth was that modern families are struggling to balance commitments to work and to family care. (This was true even for mothers on welfare, most of whom were employed in any given year, although many people viewed them as idle.) The distortion in the phrase "like other working mothers" is the idea that the struggle to balance work and family is the same for all mothers.[27]

Affluent and poor mothers face very different situations when they try to juggle paid employment and family caregiving. So do married and single mothers. A poor single mother's task of balancing commitments to provide for her children and to nurture, supervise, and protect them is extremely difficult and painful, as we commented in chapter 3. Single mothers often live in the least safe neighborhoods of a city (where they can afford rent), managing without car, savings, or insurance. They must spend a lot of time and effort to protect children from the dangers and temptations that concentrate in poor neighborhoods. Lacking money and a safe environment makes it much harder to secure work and housing, maintain a nice home, care for children, and manage the crises that occur with illness, overtime demands, layoffs, child behavior problems, and crime.[28] Take, for example, some cases reported by Stacey Oliker in her studies of work-welfare programs just before the end of AFDC.[29] Sandy is a single mother on welfare. She had managed to work full-time through her daughter's first three years, at a job that kept her poor. When the employer moved her to night shift, she continued until she feared her exhaustion was jeopardizing her daughter's safety: "There were times I come home from work and fallen asleep when she's in a tubful of water." After one such incident, she quit.[30] Now that the welfare "safety net" has ended, women like Sandy will not be able to give caregiving priority over employment, even briefly.

Cynthia had left a job to care for her mother, who was dying of cancer. Her mother had cared full-time for her young son, so, while she took care of her mother, Cynthia also now cared for her own toddler, as well as the children of an employed neighbor who paid her a small amount. Another single mother, Tina, lost a job during its probationary period, when a friend who used to walk Tina's children to the school bus stop in their high-crime neighborhood was moved to an early work shift. Tina, like many other mothers who lived in high-crime inner-city neighborhoods, never let young children walk the streets alone. Like Sandy and Cynthia, Tina had decided to favor family members' needs for care over the obligation to provide economically.

Once welfare ends, mothers like Sandy, Cynthia, and Tina will no longer be able to adapt to crises in caregiving by leaving or cutting back on their employment and depending on the safety net of welfare while they provide for children's or loved ones' needs for care. Their low wages will not allow them to buy services to substitute for those they provided for children or for the kin on whom they depend for help. Caregiving will now be an unsupported and unaffordable luxury. A low-income mother who is facing pressing family needs for care will now also face the threat that if she fails to earn, she could lose custody of children she cannot support.

The conditions of low-income single motherhood are different from the affluent working mothers we encounter in media images, who solve problems by purchasing services, taking unpaid leave, or asking husbands to help. These images obscure the kinds of resources one needs to spend "quality time" with children or to keep a child out of trouble or to help an ailing grandparent. As work and family issues get more attention from policy makers, it is essential to pay attention to the variations in families' needs for support. One size of government support will not fit all.

Government and Caregiving in Other Industrial Countries

Is It Different? Better? Less Gendered?

The breadwinner-caregiver family ideal was not unique to the United States. It became the primary family ideal and form of family organization in other industrializing countries as well. Yet, the U.S. model of social provision and support for care is a minority model in the industrialized world. Countries like England and Canada developed systems with similar features, but they provided health care and welfare to a much greater extent than we have. Other Western countries developed systems that differ strikingly from ours.[31]

So far, we have stressed the importance of "separate spheres" in shaping government care. A look at how other countries with similar gender beliefs developed more generous and egalitarian public care can show us how other factors shape government care as well. We show how other democracies progressed from offering "political citizenship" (the vote) to broader forms of "social citizenship" (universal rights to health care and welfare) than we have.[32] Social citizenship, in the form of broad supports for caregiving, has contributed to equalizing resources between men and women in many countries, in addition to providing widespread security. Most voters in these countries have a sense of collective responsibility for taking care of all citizens; this moderates their notions of individualism and family self-sufficiency.

European countries have created and maintained generous government care under conservative governments, as well as liberal or "social democratic" ones (see Exhibit 5.1). In Europe, although conservative governments have always been concerned about government eroding family authority and care, they have more willingly used government to shore up the family and keep families stable in the face of destructive economic pressures.[33] Most expansive systems of support for care—including Sweden's—also developed amid shared beliefs in male breadwinners and female caregivers.

Conservative Governments' Welfare Systems

Countries like Germany, Austria, France, and the Netherlands designed conservative programs for supporting family caregiving. They accepted the image of the breadwinner-caregiver family, and some of them aimed only to protect families, not to redistribute income from rich to poor. These countries employed a variety of arrangements to keep women at home caring for children: Some actively excluded women from the workforce, some paid benefits only through employed men. Many supported caregivers, providing child allowances (especially for large families); some even gave modest pensions to those who did unpaid care work rather than work for pay.[34]

EXHIBIT 5.1

Universal Government Supports for Families With Children (Benefits Available to All Families, Regardless of Income)

	Health Care[a]	Maternity and Parental Leave Benefits	Government-Provided Child Care	Family Allowances	Tax Relief for Children
Australia	✓	—	✓	✓	—
Austria	✓	✓	—	✓	—
Belguim	✓	✓	✓	✓	✓
Canada	✓	✓	✓	✓	✓
Denmark	✓	✓	✓	✓	—
Finland	✓	✓	✓	✓	✓
France	✓	✓	✓	✓	✓
Germany	✓	✓	✓	✓	✓
Greece	✓	✓	✓	✓	✓
Ireland	✓	✓	—	✓	—
Italy	✓	✓	✓	—	✓
Japan	✓	✓	✓	✓	✓
Luxemburg	✓	✓	✓	✓	✓
Netherlands	✓	✓	✓	✓	—
Norway	✓	✓	✓	✓	✓
Portugal	✓	✓	✓	✓	✓
Spain	✓	✓	✓	✓	✓
Sweden	✓	✓	✓	✓	—
Switzerland	✓	✓	—	✓	✓
United Kingdom	✓	✓	✓	✓	—
United States	—	—	—	—	✓

Source: Gauthier's *The State and the Family* and Navarro's *The Politics of Health Policy.*[35]
a. "Health care" in this case refers to varied systems of universal government subsidy and care.

Welfare systems built to support breadwinner-caregiver families vary in their treatment of single-mother families. Up until very recently, the Netherlands discouraged paid work for women. It continues to support maternal care at home more generously than other conservative systems. Single mothers in The Netherlands are well protected from poverty by such policies. In the other countries that promote breadwinner-

EXHIBIT 5.2

Poverty Rates of Single Mothers 20 to 55 Years Old

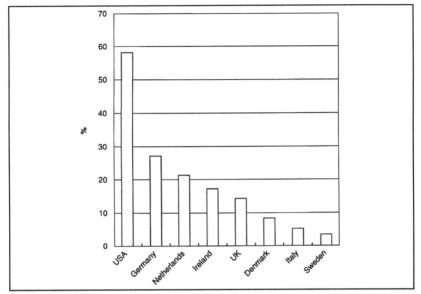

Source: Lewis's *Lone Mothers in European Welfare.*[36] Used by permission.

caregiver families, single mothers are poorer than married mothers, although they are not nearly as likely to be poor as single mothers in the United States because of government supports (see Exhibit 5.2).[37]

Conservative French governments provided family cash allowances, based on family size, to encourage families to produce more children. The breadwinner-caregiver model inspires France's policies, but when economic pressures pushed French mothers into employment, government offered all families a range of supports to stabilize family life. Under conservative and liberal governments, France developed one the most extensive systems of free, public preschool in the world.[38]

Almost all French parents, whether employed or not, take advantage of high-quality nursery schools. Programs for infants and toddlers, including family day care homes, are well-subsidized and supervised by professionals. French women are still viewed as caregivers, but a mix of policies has developed over the years that provides them with choices about home care or care for children outside the home.[39] Neither conservative politicians nor ordinary citizens try to undo this expensive program, which serves everyone and makes citizens proud of their country's care of children.

Liberal and Social Democratic Government Care

Sweden is the country most people think of when they imagine generous support for caregiving by the national government. In many ways, it is the most generous and inclusive welfare state in the world, inspired by social democratic commitments to protect working families and redistribute income and opportunities across classes. Sweden is also the system that most purposively included gender equality in its expansion of social provision, even though the breadwinner-caregiver family was its original model.

Sweden's strategy for promoting gender equality is to provide services that help women enter employment and remain in the labor force once they bear children. In addition, qualifications for benefits that allow workers to give care at home are "gender neutral," so that men can make use of supports to participate in caregiving.[40]

Gender-equalizing supports for care include 18 months of paid leave from work for birth or adoption, reimbursed at 90 percent of one's normal wage rate and extendable at lower reimbursement. Either fathers or mothers can claim the leave or they may share it between them. They are guaranteed their jobs after leave. Upon returning, they may work part-time until their youngest child is eight years old. Until a child is 12 years old, parents are entitled to 60 paid sick days a year to care for the child. Leave time counts toward pensions, rather subtracting from them. Thus giving care does not disadvantage women in old age to the extent that it does in the United States. Child care for parents who remain at work or who return is guaranteed and subsidized.

In addition to these parent-worker benefits, Sweden provides universal entitlements—in the form of allowances, subsidies, and direct services for old age, health, housing, and "lone parent" households. Most of the services, like child care and home aides, are nationally (as well as locally) funded, but they are community based in form and function. In local communities, people deliberate and participate in the design and oversight of services they receive.

As a result of such policies, nearly 9 out of 10 Swedish mothers of children under seven are in the workforce, most working part-time. On the other hand, more very young children are cared for at home by a parent in Sweden than in the United States. The reason: Swedish parents at home are still employed; they are just on leave. Although they may lose some advancement opportunities, parents who take leave forfeit very little income, and they continue to receive workplace benefits. In 8 out of 10 families with children, a parent takes nine full months of leave. It is not a risk to take one—most everyone does. Most women, that is.

Swedish fathers who stay home with young children are still a minority, even though generous leaves and government encouragement for men to use them has promoted increases in male leave taking over the decades of the policy's existence. The biggest change is the number of fathers who take some leave at childbirth and sick-child leave later on. Visitors to Sweden often comment that they see fathers with children everywhere and all the time, so the contrast with most other countries is apparent. But lengthy leave taking for caring is still a predominantly female pattern.

As in the past, Swedish women remain the primary caregivers for children. The new ideals of shared care have not yet been integrated into men's work lives. Male careers and men's peers still discourage long parental leave for men. Women do take leaves to care for infants; they then often become very attached to staying home with their children and decide to work part-time permanently. In addition, women workers flooded into the government-sponsored caregiving jobs that opened up in massive numbers when benefits were created; many of these "women's" jobs were designed to be part-time.

As a result, although the gender gap in hourly wages is small in Sweden in comparison with the United States, the workforce is at least as segregated by gender, and women bring home lower incomes than men do because they work fewer hours. These differences in men's and women's jobs probably influence most couples' decision about who should take leave for or specialize in caregiving. Compared to women in the United States, for example, Swedish women are even less well represented in the higher ranks of private industry.

The Swedish system for supporting caregiving has mixed effects on gender equality. By encouraging female employment and providing gender-neutral supports for care, Swedish policies have drawn more mothers into the workforce and more fathers into caregiving, challenging the breadwinner-caregiver family ideal. At the same time, Swedish policy has reinforced, without intending to, women's specialization in caregiving, both at home and at work. Even in Sweden, there are serious obstacles to gender equality in caregiving and earning.

Norway, Denmark, and Finland also have generous government supports for care. In each country, political struggles and the history of women's employment have shaped government programs. We described Norway's system of parental leaves and "daddy leaves" in chapter 3. Finland, more than anywhere else, has created the most choices about being a full-time caregiver or combining earning and caring. In comparison with Sweden, Finland has more women who stay home to rear children past infancy and who receive significant support to do so. Yet, Finnish parents who choose to be employed have leave policies and day care subsidies to help them balance caregiving and paid work.[41]

Most governments provide less support for caregiving than the Scandinavian countries do. However, virtually all industrialized countries use government more extensively than we do to bolster caregiving, both inside and outside the family. The result (as well as the cause) is stronger support for government care than we find among U.S. citizens.

Caregiving and Gender Equality

Countries that support caregiving have, intentionally or unintentionally, also advanced gender equality by giving more economic security to mothers at home, taking some of the burden of care off women who are employed, or encouraging men to do more caregiving. Strategies of bringing men actively into the realm of care have been least often tried, however, and their progress has been uneven and slow. As a result, across the range of countries with bigger systems of government-supported care, women remain primary caregivers at home even when they are employed. In addition, women are the main paid caregivers, and caregiving jobs are poorly paid. Both patterns maintain gender inequality in the public realm of employment and politics, as well as at home.

In the European examples, we have seen two government strategies of improving and rewarding caregiving: *carer citizen* policies and *carer worker citizen* policies.[42] Carer citizen policies directly reward caregivers with citizen benefits—for example, old age pensions to people who care for children or elders full-time at home. These policies recognize the social contribution of caregiving by providing at least some benefits directly to caregivers, not just to caregivers through breadwinners.

Carer worker citizen policies reward citizens who combine earning and caring. These policies include parental leaves and day care. Some

European countries emphasize one strategy, some use both. All also offer *worker citizen* policies, the primary strategy of the U.S. welfare system, which is to reward breadwinners and their dependents.

Worker citizen policies and carer citizen policies are most likely to reinforce gender inequality because they encourage men to specialize in earning money and women to focus on unpaid family caregiving. But carer citizen policies also benefit women by giving public services, cash payments, and recognition to family caregivers, who are overwhelmingly women in all countries. Carer worker citizenship policies are least likely to reinforce full-time caregiving for women and are most supportive of women and men sharing earning and caring. They promote, but do not ensure, gender equality. The success of carer worker citizen policies in effecting gender equality depends on how well policies, along with other social forces, bring men actively into domestic and paid care.

Government support of caregiving, and thus support for gender equity, is increasingly threatened in Europe, as well as America, because of current economic conditions and political movements opposing welfare programs. When countries cut back their welfare provision, people with fewer resources lose care, and women lose avenues to equity. In Europe, however, broad popular support protects the welfare state, encouraging people to support higher taxes or other social costs to protect caregiving. Still, in every country, some people express concern that growth in government threatens family care.

The Threat of "Big Brother"

Throughout the twentieth century, government involvement in caregiving expanded at every level—from local to national. Some care-oriented laws and policies, like the eight-hour day and Social Security, have been very popular. Others, like welfare, never gained widespread support in the United States. Ominous portrayals of the dangers of big government have always echoed in public debates in the United States about the role of government in caregiving. The concern is that government will become a "Big Brother" who will usurp control of people's lives and sap their will to provide good care in the family or within communities.

In American debates about government support for care, three arguments against government involvement stand out: First, government bureaucracies cannot deliver genuine care. Second, government provision undermines family caregiving. Third, government undermines religious teaching. We will describe each of these arguments about "Big Brother" care and present some counterarguments.

Bureaucratic Impersonality and Personal Caring

According to some opponents of "Big Brother" care, government bureaucracy makes good care impossible, whether government provides care or subsidizes it, because of legal reasoning and bureaucratic organization. Laws are based on universal principles of fairness that require impartial decisions and general rules, but good caregiving requires serving the particular needs of individuals. Bureaucratic hierarchy and rigid rules set by distant officials also prevent caregivers from being responsive to the needs of individuals. Thus when caregiving is directed by government policies and carried out by people who must follow these policies, the needs of the person cared for and the caring feelings and behaviors of caregivers only get in the way of bureaucratic goals. Crescent Home, a nursing home described in Chapter 4, illustrates some of the negative effects that federal regulations and bureaucracy can have on caregiving.

Chapter 4 also showed that bureaucracy can have positive effects on caregiving. Government-supported organizations are required to use impartial fairness principles in deciding who to serve and who to hire as caregivers. They can also enforce policies that assure humane working conditions, such as worker-safety rules, and rules that protect care receivers, such as regulations that have effectively minimized physical abuse in nursing homes.

The positive potential effects of bureaucracy are illustrated in Chapter 4 by the Clinical Practice Model of nursing. Though it has some problems, the model shows how bureaucracy can significantly improve caregiving if rules and procedures emphasize nurses' interpersonal skills and the time requirements of caring. Large-scale bureaucracies can give paid workers the time, training, autonomy and resources to do their caregiving tasks well.

Of course, even with such changes, bureaucratic care rarely involves the deep and long-term personal commitments characteristic of family or friendship relationships, but it can still be a sympathetic, other-oriented relationship that meets many of the care receivers' needs.

Another way bureaucracies can ensure that caregiving meets the needs of those being cared for is by involving clients and members of their communities in decision making and oversight. In the United States, nonprofit social service organizations sometimes do this. In Swedish municipalities, community members and child care users supervise day care centers that receive considerable funding and basic guidelines from national government. By giving authority to care receivers and community members, centralized or large-scale organizations can accomplish their caregiving missions more efficiently.

Opponents of government provision argue that bureaucratic organizations cannot deliver good care. Our response is that bureaucracy presents obstacles to responsive caregiving, but many obstacles can be removed by rules and procedures that fit the requirements of caregiving.

Government and
the Institution of Family Care

The second major criticism of government support for caregiving focuses on preserving the family. According to this argument, as soon as larger social institutions provide or regulate care, the new alternatives weaken the institution of the family and its capacity to care. It is not just that government programs deliver poor care; they also undermine the family as a primary institution of care. When government provides alternate models of care and alternate choices for care receivers, individuals become too independent of families, and families become fragile.

For example, if government regulates parents' use of physical punishment, then children learn to turn to government authorities, as well as to their parents, for protection and care. As children become less dependent on their family, parents have less authority to impose their desired forms of caregiving. Families have a harder time reinforcing their members' commitments to caring for one another; giving care is a more avoidable obligation. Because of government-supported services, the family becomes a less predictable and stable institution of care.

This argument focuses on the ways widespread family patterns are institutionalized—that is, reinforced by social expectations and social sanctions and taken for granted by family members. When government creates other places than the family where one can be cared for, it is harder for communities to pressure families to care. Families can avoid what some might consider their duty to care for a disabled child, saying, "Let the government take care of him!" Family members can no longer count on receiving approval for the dedication to others, altruism, and self-sacrifice that caregiving involves. A preferable guide to living becomes "Hey, it's time to look out for number one!" Alternative forms of care may deinstitutionalize the family's obligation to care and families' capacities to give care.

Many who use the institutional argument point to the ease with which increasing numbers of men divorce their wives and abandon their children. They argue that liberal divorce laws or the ability of divorced wives to live on welfare have made it easier for fathers to opt out of their traditional obligation to provide for their families.

Has the expansion of government provision resulted in a general decline in family care? The evidence shows variable, not uniform, effects. The decline in fathers providing for their family may partly result from government supports for caregiving. On the other hand, some researchers have concluded that government has bolstered or extended family bonds in families that could not maintain caregiving without outside support. For example, welfare enabled single mothers to keep their children and raise them rather than send them into institutional care. In the early part of the century, a majority of children in orphanages actually had a living parent, usually a mother who could not economically support them.[43] Although some people disapprove, others see an expansion of family care when mothers who are deserted or who bear children outside of marriage can keep and care for their children.

Government support for paid, nonfamily caregiving can also bolster family care. High-quality government-supported day care centers can relieve the pressures on overwhelmed family caregivers so they can enjoy their caring work more and do it better. Employed parents with reliable day care are likely to be more relaxed when they are home and likely to be more attentive to their children. Similarly, a daughter caring for a severely disabled elderly parent probably will provide better care if she can occasionally turn over her care work to a government-subsidized homeworker while she goes out with her friends.

Social Security and other government "safety nets" for the old or unemployed can strengthen connections with a wide network of kin by reducing the financial risk of staying connected. Historians have offered surprising evidence that, in the past, people did not value large networks of affectionate and caring relatives until they could build close relations without risking economic responsibility for them.[44] In addition, families relieved of physical caregiving often have time to do more emotional caring with elders, children, and even spouses.

Another way that government programs strengthen families is through laws and regulations that increase time for family caregiving. As we described above, policies like the eight-hour day and paid work leaves for dependent care give families more time to provide care at home. Many European countries with big welfare states have more parents at home with young children than the United States does with its much smaller welfare state. Parental care is financially supported by government-subsidized work leaves or family care allowances.

The impact of government on the family is variable, not uniformly supportive or destructive, as we can see by comparing government provision in different nations and in different times. The effects of government on family care depend on a number of economic, cultural, institutional, and historic circumstances. This means a policy's impact on families may differ, not only among countries, or over time, but among groups within a country as well.

The impact of government on the quality of caregiving inside and outside the family depends, in large part, on how responsive government is to the needs of different groups and to caregivers and care receivers. It depends on how accountable the government program is to citizens and on how effectively the interpersonal relations and time requirements of caregiving are recognized and built into laws and government policy and programs.

The element of the antigovernment argument that we can not at all disprove is that government-supported care gives people choices, and choices can weaken institutions in some ways. Government support has allowed people to decline to care or to delegate care (the availability of paid care has a similar effect on affluent families). Government may have relieved families of the stresses of the most burdensome caregiving, but it has also made it easier for men and women to leave marriages and to leave children.

People need neither to marry nor have children to be cared for in sickness and old age. Neither marriage nor child rearing is as compulsory as it once was. Government may help families to care, but, in some ways, it makes it harder to enforce family caregiving. The traditional patterns of marriage and the family are not as taken for granted and routine as they once were, and government policies and programs have probably contributed to this change.

Even if government provision has helped to weaken the compulsory and uniform dimensions of the family institution, however, it has also encouraged the development of diverse kinds of caregiving families. Although the compulsory breadwinner-caregiver form of family has been weakened as a taken-for-granted pattern for everyone, other forms of familial caregiving may be becoming institutionalized as government-supported care expands.

In the context of changing laws and an expanding welfare state, families with single parents have become increasingly viable and increasingly accepted as legitimate families (though acceptance is far from universal). Networks of kin and close friends who exchange family-supporting care across households are receiving more respect and recognition. Gay and lesbian couples, especially those rearing children, are gaining acceptance as families. Law and policy can give legitimacy to different family forms, as the current intense political struggle over legal marriage for same-sex couples illustrates.

Although only the single-mother form of family care is well on its way to becoming institutionalized, in terms of broad legitimacy and integration into policies and laws, these other family formations may be on their way. We expect to see changes in acknowledged family roles—for example, family benefits for a grandmother who lives alone but provides daily, "parental" care; legal parental rights for a nonbiological comother who is lesbian; a caregiver allowance for a neighbor who manages the household and finances of an elder who would otherwise live in a nursing home. Government support of caregiving may help to deinstitutionalize the breadwinner-caregiver family, but it has also helped to institutionalize new forms of family caregiving.

Government Care and Religious Authority

A third argument used by opponents of government involvement in caregiving is that it violates the teachings of religion. Some religions teach that caregiving is the sacred duty of mothers and that economic provision and leadership is the sacred duty of fathers. They see government-sponsored care as an intrusion that undermines the sacred order of families and that weakens religious community. Some religions oppose policies of child protection against abuse because it limits parents' authority in child discipline. Some oppose legal divorce because it allows men or women to abandon the sacrament of marriage and evade family obligations. Some oppose welfare because it enables mothers to head families without fathers. The idea underlying these kinds of religious opposition to government is that policies and laws like these encourage people to reject the family values their religion teaches.

Government authority *does* undermine the authority of religion in people's lives. Laws and policies to protect children limit a parent's ability to impose harsh discipline. Legal divorce and other policies multiply alternatives available to individual family members, which makes it harder for religious communities to enforce some teachings. Religious authority is limited to faithful followers.

On the other hand, government also protects freedom of religion. In a society with many different religions and, thus, diverse beliefs about right and wrong, government authority can ensure the right to practice whatever religion a person may choose. Government laws and policies can limit the authority of any one religion to regulate everyone's family lives, but it allows many religions to flourish and serve the families of their believers.

In the end, your conclusions about the role of government in care will likely depend on your personal beliefs about what a family, government, and caregiving should be and how much responsibility you believe citizens have to help care for people outside their own family.

We have argued that bureaucratic government services can both interfere with good care and improve caregiving. Government provision changes the family, but some of these changes strengthen families. Government laws both limit the authority of religion and protect freedom of religion. Depending on your values, you might see these effects of government support for caregiving as undermining families and the quality of care, or you might see them as renewing families by giving support, legitimacy, and stability to diverse family formations and improving the quality of caregiving.

How Can Government Both Support Caregiving and Promote Gender Equality?

Let us assume, for the moment, that government laws and policies can effectively support good caregiving, inside and outside of families. Can this support be combined with increasing gender equality? Developing government programs that move our society toward both gender equality and better care is very challenging. It would be much easier to imagine how government could simply promote gender equality by encouraging less caregiving and helping women do less caring—paid or unpaid. Women could then compete with men on a more level playing field, as workers or citizens freed of responsibility to care for others. This route to gender equality would probably be unappealing to most men and women, however, because it would greatly reduce caregiving. On the other hand, programs that focus only on supporting caregiving, like child allowances, risk reenforcing the existing gender division of breadwinning and caregiving.

Policies can foster both caregiving and gender equality only if they encourage men as well as women to be caregivers. The government policies for gender-equitable caregiving that we have discussed in this chapter use four strategies of supporting care:

1. They support paid care outside the family;
2. they increase social recognition of caregiving—both paid and un-paid—as productive and valuable work;
3. they make caregiving more economically rewarding or less economically costly to caregivers; and
4. they challenge the idea that caregiving is naturally the work of women, not men.

We consider these strategies below.

Supporting Caregiving Outside the Family

The availability of care outside the family is distinctly important for gender equality because it gives women choices about family caregiving. Mothers abandoned the role of acute nursing care when hospital nursing began to provide good care. Government support of hospitals—or, for another example, public schooling—enabled women to be earners as well as caregivers. It also enabled mothers to increase their emotional, as opposed to physical, caregiving.

Government supports were especially important resources for those women who had to earn but whose low earnings would not enable them to pay for private hospitals or schools. Such supports enriched care for those families who would have had to do without care. Government supports were especially important resources for wives whose husbands resisted their entry into employment. When hospitals and elementary schools were widely recognized as providing good care, wives had these social sources of persuasion to use to counter husbands' demands that they stay home to care.

Social Recognition of Caregiving

Laws, policies, and programs can increase societywide recognition of the worth of caregiving and raise its status and value. Examples of how government can support and raise the status of unpaid caregiving are scattered throughout this chapter. Early twentieth-century maternalists in the United States wanted mothers' pensions to reward the social contribution of maternal caregiving. Contemporary Dutch welfare policies generously subsidize maternal care of children at home, narrowing the poverty gap between men and women. Swedish policies recognize that earners are also caregivers, make it easier for caregivers to be earners, and encourage men to earn and care along with women.

Government policies have raised the status of paid caregiving by recognizing and certifying the skills involved. We found a remarkable example of progress in recognizing and rewarding low-wage caregivers' skills in a little-known government child care program. The U.S. Army sponsors the largest "employer-sponsored" child care in the country, serving 200,000 children in centers, family care homes, and other programs. In the 1980s, the Army quietly but forcefully began a program to improve the quality of its child care system. Army regulations require each installation to offer an on-the-job training program for child caregivers.[45]

Entering jobs with the minimal education credentials of most child care providers, Army caregivers progress through a series of training segments by demonstrating caregiving skills and knowledge on the job. Each level of competence is associated with increases in pay and responsibility. The process recognizes, teaches, and rewards the development of skills in caregiving. The Child Development Associate Credential is usable inside and outside the military services. Some colleges offer credit toward advanced degrees to its holders.[46]

The Army strategy of improving care involved recognizing, teaching, and rewarding the skills of child caregiving. On-the-job learning was formalized in ways that improved the social status of caregivers and gave them opportunities for advancement on the job or into higher status caregiving careers through further education.

Another way that government has recognized paid caregiving is with "comparable worth" policies that compare and rank government jobs equitably. By improving the job evaluation systems used to decide skill and pay levels, governments have reranked low-level female-dominated jobs, such as licenced practical nurse, to reflect levels of skill, effort, and training that are comparable to those of higher ranked male-dominated jobs, such as corrections counselor.[47] Comparable worth policies spread recognition of caregiving skills and help to raise wages for care work.

In the Army's child care program and comparable worth policies, the government, as a large employer, serves as a model for private sector employers. Government can, however, also regulate private sector employment in ways that equitably recognize care. For example, requiring state licenses and special training for "psych techs" improved the quality of care at a hospital for people with severe mental retardation, as we described in chapter 4. Requiring day care training and licensure and regulating the numbers of children supervised by each day care worker both recognizes the worth of care and improves its quality. Similar policies could benefit nurses' aides in nursing homes.

Rewarding Caregiving and Limiting Its Costs

The Army's day care training and states' comparable worth policies are examples of both recognizing and rewarding caregiving. Improvements in wages for paid caregiving depend, in large part, on recognizing the effort, skill, and training involved in care. In both child care and health care, pressures to lower labor costs might mean that government subsidy of wages or of consumer costs would be necessary, in addition to regulation.

Examples of policies that limit the costs of giving unpaid care have been abundant in this chapter. The U.S. Family and Medical Leave Act requires large companies to preserve the jobs of new parents who take unpaid leave to care. European countries take parental leave giant steps forward in reducing the costs of care by extending the leaves and paying salaries during leave. By mandating numerous sick days that parents can use for dependent care, they reduce the costs to one's career of the normal demands of caregiving. Governments also reduce the cost of caregiving when they make old age pensions a right of all citizens, including homemakers as well as breadwinners. Divorce laws reduce the costs of caregiving when they require settlements that compensate for the lost wages and leisure of caregivers. Child custody laws reduce the costs of caregiving when they require noncustodial parents to contribute equitably to the support of children.

Revising Gendered Notions of Care

Recognizing and rewarding the effort and skills involved in care dissolves the idea that caring is a natural characteristic of women. Recognizing, rewarding, and lessening the economic costs of care are probably the best ways government can revise gendered ideas about caregiving. These strategies make caregiving more appealing to those who previously benefited only by avoiding it. They make caregiving more appealing to men, whose participation revises gendered notions.

The Nordic countries, especially Sweden, provide examples of how governments directly attempt to revise gendered notions of care. There, caregiving is a primary mission of government institutions, along with the previously "masculine" domains of warfare, law, and order.[48] They designed "parental," not "maternal," leaves to encourage men to share family care. When men used leaves significantly less than women because of ongoing social incentives for breadwinning over caregiving, Norway installed special incentives for fathers to take leaves. Paternal leaves are brief, so they may have little effect on the long-term division of caregiving labor at home. Many Norwegians, though, believe they are seeing the beginning of a new ethic and new patterns of paternal involvement in care. If they are right, then we have an example of how government may directly help to "ungender" care.

Must We Ungender Care to Make Men and Women Social Equals?

Each of these strategies of recognizing, rewarding, and revising the gendered images of care helps to encourage men's caregiving and improves caregiving in general. We have seen, however, that it may be easier for government policy to improve the prestige and quality of caregiving than to encourage men to do it. Sweden is a powerful example of this limitation, for in spite of gender-neutral policies making leaves and part-time work available to men who elect to care, men use them far less than women do. Sweden has increased men's involvement in caregiving, but there are no signs that men are becoming equal caregivers. Indeed, gender-neutral policies seem to have helped sharpen the distinctions between men's and women's employment and care patterns: women remained the primary domestic caregivers while they swelled the fast-growing sector of paid care in Sweden.

The Swedish case—and the U.S. experience of massive changes in women's participation in the workplace along with small changes in men's domestic care—suggest a question that a modern-day maternalist might ask: cannot men and women become social equals while specializing, respectively, in breadwinning and caregiving? The question is compelling, partly because current patterns convince so many people that women are, indeed, better at caring and partly because the gendered pattern has been so resistant to change. Our sociological perspective, however, suggests the answer is no—although government can help reduce the disparity, women and men cannot become social equals if women remain the caregiver group.

We maintain that equality requires sharing the satisfactions and burdens of caregiving because caregiving will always exact costs in individual power and privilege, and the costs are unlikely to be balanced even by good government supports for care. For one thing, it is probably impossible to create an economic "yardstick" for care that translates the rewards of a market economy into an equal system of rewards for nonmarket caring. Even if yardsticks were developed and all family and community caregiving were somehow paid, this would undercut the altruistic moral meanings of care. Most people's images of a good society involve considerable amounts of voluntary, unselfish caring.

Secondly, and more practically, even wealthy welfare states could not afford to pay for all the care most people seem to want. Good paid caregiving requires trained, highly motivated workers who devote enough time to responding to the individual needs of care receivers. Thus, good paid caregiving is expensive, unprofitable in most situations, and, for both reasons, requires government support. Practically, as well as morally, most ideals of a good society require considerable unpaid care.

In sum, government care can make caring more honorable and rewarding and can influence gender patterns of care, but supports to caregivers will not be *sufficient* to make primary caregivers the equals of primary breadwinners or to encourage massive changes in men's caregiving activities. To the extent that breadwinning remains a richer source of honor, privilege, and social power, and to the degree that caregiving constrains access to power and privilege, men are likely to delegate primary caregiving to women.

If men currently have the resources of power and belief that enable them to delegate primary caregiving to women, how can government help to shift that balance? How might law and government policy and programs affect cultural beliefs and families' private struggles over caregiving?

- First, government can curb the demands of the marketplace in ways that give families more time for care. For example, law and policy can redefine the normal work day. Earlier laws that established an eight-hour day redefined the norms of work in a way that fit the breadwinner-caregiver ideal. A shift to a six-hour work day, paid as full-time, would redefine the norms of work to better fit the newer ideal of parents who earn and care. A six-hour day would make it easier for men and women to combine earning and caring. Moreover, it would make it easier for individual women to demand a shift of male attention from earning to caring.

- Laws and policies can empower women to make effective demands on men's domestic time. Research shows that employed wives secure more domestic help from husbands, especially in couples employed a similar number of hours. This suggests that employment policy might be at least as important as care supports for getting men to share caring work at home. Comparable worth policies that require equal pay for work of comparable skill and effort would enable employed mothers more often to bring home salaries comparable to their mates and give them strengthened bargaining power over the division of care. Economic supports for single-mother families make the possibility of living independently a bargaining resource for wives.

- Laws and policies can increase the individual costs of evading care and change cultural expectations about men's caregiving. Divorce, paternity, and child custody decisions could recognize the life-long costs of intensive caregiving for children and assure that non-caregivers share the costs fairly. Old age pensions could do the same. Government policy can thus sanction the failure to care as well as recognize and reward care. Currently, men pay penalties at work for putting family first. Policy that sanctions noncaregivers spreads the social costs in a way that also stigmatizes the failure to care.

Conclusion

Government action has been and will be an important influence on caregiving. Laws, policies, and programs shape the meanings of care;

they support, regulate, and apportion responsibility for caregiving. We have seen how policy and programs that incorporated the breadwinner-caregiver family ideal became the foundation of the U.S. government's involvement in care. Building on this foundation, the United States created a two-tiered welfare system that treats breadwinners as entitled citizens and caregivers as dependents.

The United States stands alone among the industrialized democracies of the world in its meager government supports for caregiving, even though other countries were also influenced by the breadwinner-caregiver ideal. Beliefs about the role of government in family life and caregiving have made Americans especially hostile to government care.

To question beliefs that government can only undermine families and caregiving, we have considered how government care can support rather than subvert family care and how institutions can provide good care. Indeed, citizens could use government both to extend care and to move toward gender equality. Laws, policies, and programs can challenge the idea that caregiving is naturally women's work; they can recognize the value of paid and unpaid caregiving; they can support good care outside, as well as inside, the family; and they can make good caregiving more rewarding to caregivers. A component of these strategies is to bring men, as well as women, into the routines and responsibilities of caregiving.

Of course, government policy alone will not effect a shift in gender patterns of care. Changes in the private sector, widespread individual efforts, and movements that change ideas are essential for expanding caregiving and encouraging or constraining men to do it. In the concluding chapter, we consider how such coordinated efforts could both improve caregiving and move our society towards gender equality. Historically, government changes have more often followed after family and cultural changes than led them. Yet, sometimes, government policies helped to change beliefs, for example in the case of civil rights for minorities.

Widespread changes in the social status of caregivers cannot simply be legislated. People give care and think about care in their particular families and communities. This chapter has concentrated on how government provides resources for people to make changes. The next one looks at how people organize voluntarily, in their communities, to care. We address a question often raised by opponents of government programs for caregiving: Cannot community programs and volunteers do a better job than the government in supporting caregiving?

CHAPTER 6

Caregiving in Communities

In Milwaukee, Wisconsin, members of a Methodist congregation stay in close touch with the church's elderly members, taking them meals when they are ill, putting up winter storm windows, and chauffeuring them to church.

In Charlotte, North Carolina, Black and White members of a broad array of city churches, neighborhoods, and community groups meet to figure out how to support the families of single mothers facing the end of welfare. In addition to asking for government programs to address family needs, they are devising ways to multiply sources of shelter and child care, using homes and churches as sites for emergency care.

In San Francisco, California, volunteers who were formerly unacquainted members of a loose-knit gay community mobilized to provide care for men who were sick with or dying of AIDS. Making commitments to daily care, volunteers developed intense attachments to care receivers. These commitments and attachments greatly increased the gay community's capacities to provide care and to advocate politically for supports for care.

These are a few examples of caregiving that takes place in communities. Most people like the idea of giving and receiving care within a community. The idea of community is an idea about belonging among people who know one another and who care about and feel responsible to each other. We often think of community care as given out of a real sense of "caring about" others with whom we share a sense of commitment. A community's shared obligations and dependability tie people to each other, even outside the family. In this chapter, we first define the meaning of community care and then explore its benefits and limitations.

What Is Community Care?

Communities of Place, Network, and Identity

The word "community" usually refers to a local, geographical place where people feel a sense of membership and belonging.[1] In this sense, a community may be a city, a district, or a neighborhood. Community caregiving in a local place may take forms like a homeless shelter, a children's recreation program, or a Meals on Wheels program. It may take place in less formally organized ways; for example, when neighbors shovel snow at the homes of elderly neighbors or when a neighborhood elder keeps an eye on the street where children are at play.

The word community may also indicate a group or network or identity community, instead of a place—a Jewish community, for example, or a gay community, or an Italian community. This kind of community may not be geographically bounded.[2] It usually involves people who share a common identity or who work or worship together. Sometimes the community meets in a place, like a church. Sometimes the community is formed by a number of shared practices or places of interaction—for example, a gay community without gay neighborhoods, which brings people together in a number of places or associations.

Whether they are based in places, networks, or common identities, communities involve a sense of common membership, belonging, and commitment. They also involve people who meet each other (or who feel they might meet each other) in face-to-face relationships.[3]

Voluntary and Paid Community Care

For many people, the term *community care* means voluntary, unpaid care. Some think the distinction between paid care and unpaid care is important because they believe that, as with families, real care is voluntary, not paid. Yet, many caregivers at the level of community are paid to care by a community group or government. For example, some staff at a battered women's shelter might receive wages. A community-based project might be funded by government. An elder care program might pay allowances to relatives or neighbors to provide regular care.

Voluntary and unpaid care can be more purely altruistic than paid care, so the moral characteristic of altruism may give voluntary care a unique value. Yet, this book has shown how women, in particular, are channeled and pressured into what appears to be voluntary care, so their sacrifices for others may not always be freely chosen. We have also shown how payment that enables a committed caregiver to divert time from earning to caring enables care where there would otherwise be none. For example, a neighbor who must work for pay might accept a caregiver's allowance to help the elder next door avoid a nursing home. In addition, we have suggested that limited caring relationships are important sources of care—even preferable, at times, to a fully developed relation of care. For all these reasons, we will include paid care in our conception of community care.

Care in communities is sometimes supported by funding from noncommunity sources. The goals and interests of noncommunity groups may influence the ways communities care when community groups become dependent on outside funding or when funders impose rules on the use of funds or, simply, when they fund some but not other kinds of projects. In these cases, the funding of community caregiving organizations often blurs the lines between community group and government, private foundations, or business.[4] The funding and regulation of community care complicates the meanings of community care, just as paying for care does. But the meanings of care by those with whom one feels a sense of community justify exploring this kind of caregiving, in spite of its complexity.

Our focus in this chapter is on voluntary care. We emphasize how voluntary care for others who are part of our communities supports care within families and contributes to a caring society. We also consider how our society elicits and rewards community care. Answering this question leads us, once again, to gender asymmetries in caregiving and the gendered character of voluntary care.

What Are the Benefits of Care in Communities?

Whether we think of communities as local places or as networks of relationships, care within communities can have some unique, beneficial characteristics. We can find advantages to community care in both its paid and its volunteer forms.

Community Caregiving Can Be Communal

Community caregiving can offer intimacy, familiarity, long commitment, trust, and belonging to both care receivers and caregivers. When a caregiver and a care receiver who do not know each other personally feel a common bond—perhaps each may know someone who knows the other—this contributes to a feeling of trust in the care exchange. It also contributes to a sense of being part of a wider and more reciprocal circle of care. The care receiver may imagine "giving back" to the community some day and so receiving care may feel less like charity. The caregiver may become a care receiver in the same community. Being members of the same community, the act of care is part of a larger series of exchanges, a web of familiarity, reciprocation, trust, and belonging.

When these qualities of intimacy and long commitment are present, community care has "communal" qualities, like those that encourage people to value the family as the central site of caregiving. Communal qualities can make community caregiving powerful in the effects and meanings it has for participants and for their communities. Communal relationships outside the family can extend and enrich family caregiving by providing encouragement, supports, and supplements.

Communal care may be especially valuable to people without families or whose families do not meet their needs for care or allow them to give care. A church's meal program, for example, can provide moments of homelike comfort to homeless people or those who have no kin. Familiarity and caring among meal program regulars, both helpers and participants, nourishes beyond nutrition. Similarly, a community center for gay teenagers can provide the understanding confidants, accessible role models, and resources for self-esteem that angry parents or ignorant friends fail to offer. For some people, community institutions provide care better than their families do.

Just as communities may encourage communal qualities of care, communal qualities of care build community. Among people who are not family, caregiving that creates interdependence and deepens familiarity, trust, and commitment has a community-building meaning beyond the caring relationship.

Community Care
Can Be Familiar

Caregiving that is oriented to particular communities can enrich care by incorporating local conditions and customs. Food and recreation in a rural nursing home will probably satisfy residents without the variety a big-city home would need to meet its diverse residents' needs, but rural residents may need more space and more opportunities to garden and work with animals. Children in day care may take special comfort and joy when their parents and teachers cooperate to bring in each child's cultural celebrations or family customs to share.

Community Care Can Be Constructively "In Between"

The sense of familiarity, trust, belonging, and mutual obligation gives care in a community some of the qualities of care in a family. Yet communities are larger than families. They envelop families and can support caregiving inside them. The African proverb "It takes a village to raise a child" recognizes how important committed others are to accomplishing family goals. The communal "village" surrounding a family may be close friends who help parents solve child-rearing problems or who help a wife figure out how to change her marriage. It may be an organization that sponsors a family crisis hotline or a program of after-school supervision.

Communities are larger than families but smaller than governments. They can mediate between families and government; for example, by representing the needs of families in the policy arena. Community care can buffer individuals and families from the harsh effects of government policy or the economic marketplace.[5] For example, local groups can mobilize their members to replenish food banks when government cuts leave more people hungry. Parishes may organize their own child care centers when economic pressures force more parents to work long hours. Community provision of food and child care has enabled local workers to sustain strikes for higher wages and enabled local activists to sustain boycotts and sit-ins on behalf of civil rights.

Community caregiving, even within organizations, may be created closer to the needs of those cared for than care that is designed nationally or in a large service industry. Often, it is less uniform and bureaucratic than government or for-profit care. Often, it is experienced as more "organic," "grassroots," or democratic.

The responsiveness of community caregiving can be undermined when government funds community efforts and then regulates them. The line between government and community care can become blurred in this way. Even so, government programs that have community-based components of decision making, oversight, and delivery can incorporate many advantages of community caregiving. Sweden's extensive system of government-sponsored child care, for example, is largely controlled at the community level, where parents and community members shape the services and oversee them.

Community Carers Can Innovate, Raise Standards, and Expand Citizenship

The "in-between-ness" of communities often allows them to pioneer needs-based innovations in care. Care receivers can draw upon their community support to increase their authority and voice in caregiving arrangements. Volunteers or paid caregivers in community-based organizations often have more autonomy to change or experiment with caregiving services. The innovations they create can be "tested" at the community level and then influence policy and practice beyond the community. Programs that are now widespread, like shelters for battered women, after-school care for children, and respite care for dependent elders were pioneered at the community level.

Community caregiving experience, in association with other people, can lead to deliberation, moral influence, and political action on behalf of extending care. In the familiar and local sites of community, caregivers easily become care advocates and policy makers. For example, people who deliver Meals on Wheels may enter the homes of frail elders, talk to them, and learn about diverse needs among elders trying to maintain their independence. Talking with members of their organization, they might develop new ideas about how their community could help with care beyond food delivery and propose a new service to the city council.

Informally helping others in the community can follow the same path linking caregiving with democratic deliberation and activism. Mary Pardo's study of the community organization, "Mothers of East Los Angeles," shows how Mexican American women who had previously been politically inactive transformed "networks and resources based on family and culture into political assets to defend the quality of urban life." Networks of friendship and acquaintance among mothers who met while participating in their children's school overlapped with neighborhood networks and became a political force to stop the building of a prison in their community.[6]

Caregiving experience, along with deliberation about good care, can also lead to change through interpersonal moral influence. The volunteers who begin talking about their experience with Meals on Wheels may discover that previously unneighborly neighbors have begun to help the elder next door. Community activists may notice that legislators need less convincing than they once did that poor children need after-school care.

The examples above, showing how giving care can be linked with policy making, also show how communities can be fertile sites for cultivating a broader definition of citizenship—one that recognizes the social value of care. Community settings are appealing and comfortable places for giving care, discussing care with others, and acting to make change. That makes them a good social space for inviting people who have not been active citizens into civic participation. Community settings could become the places where the social contributions of caregiving become widely recognized and reconceived as a service of citizenship. Where caregiving is visible, valued, and woven into policy debates, we could begin to frame caregiving as an activity of citizenship, worthy of citizen benefits.

In summary, community caregiving has benefits for individual caregivers and care receivers and for families within communities. Care in the community can be more responsive to local needs and be more comforting and familiar. Community caregiving builds community commitment and belonging. It can spark community deliberation, collective action, and needs-based innovation. It can also enlarge the terrain of good citizenship. We must also ask, though, about the disadvantages of care in communities and the limits of community caring in providing for a society's needs.

What Are the Limits of
Caregiving in Communities?

Inequities of Needs and Resources

The most serious limit of the community as a locus of caregiving is that communities vary tremendously in their needs and their resources. Communities with unusually great needs for caregiving help are often the same ones with unusually low levels of resources.

In inner-city communities, for example, poverty produces many unmet needs for health care, child care, elder care, and basic safety and survival. Inner-city needs are great, and resources are scarcer than in other urban communities. Poverty is concentrated because so many affluent people have moved to suburbs. Generally, suburban residents donate money to their own local schools, volunteer their time to community organizations close to home, and use their educational and professional skills to enrich civic efforts of their own communities.[7]

Most charitable donations of time and money stay in the communities of the contributors, so those communities that have the most become richer in caregiving resources; those that have least become poorer. Most of charitable giving, even within cities, is for religious groups that do not spend most of their funds on social services.[8]

Poor communities are richer in informal helping, among kin or in neighborhoods, than in formal caregiving, through organizations.[9] Large numbers of people who reside in inner cities are overburdened by the need to give care in their families or by informal helping among friends and neighbors. Their time and energies are devoted to informal caregiving that is part of daily survival. Many lack the time, money, experience, and social contacts to form community caregiving organizations that can draw support from outside the community to meet the community's needs. Fewer formally organized efforts also means fewer ways that caregivers can influence policy making.

Community Care Can Be Humiliating or Coercive

A second shortcoming of care in communities is that care receivers may experience some kinds of community care, like some kinds of family care, as particularly humiliating or as an excessive burden to others. Those of us who dislike impersonal or bureaucratic care might sometimes prefer it to charitable services from people we know in our communities. We might not want people in our own communities to witness our crises of economic failure, disability, or dependence. Like the disabled people we discussed in chapter 4, we might feel that our debt of gratitude to helpers places us in a subordinate relation to people to whom we want to feel equal.

Paradoxically, the same communal qualities of familiarity and mutual obligation that can establish a positive sense of belonging can also create a negative sense of surveillance and control. Community is not always an ideal site of care.

Community Care Can Discriminate

A third limitation of community-based care is that it may discriminate against groups or individuals who differ from the community's dominant group. The "we" feeling that can be so beneficial in community care usually does not extend evenly throughout a community. Religious or racial minorities may be treated as outsiders instead of members; for example, when a community elders program celebrates only Christmas and not Rosh Hashannah or Ramadan. In general, it is difficult to have a strong we feeling without excluding others.

Cultural differences may be misunderstood and needs thus overlooked: School officials might interpret a grandmother's presence at teacher-parent meetings as a sign of parental neglect, when overseeing schoolwork is just this "other mother's " regular child-rearing respon-sibility. Some household forms, such as single-parent families or dou-bling up in housing to prevent homelessness, may mark people as unworthy of the benefits of community care.

Community Care Can
Reinforce Gender Inequality

One of the least noticed limitations of care in communities is that it is gendered. The gendering of community-based caregiving reveals the patterns we have seen in other contexts. Community care is shaped by beliefs that women's caregiving is natural. In communities, as in fami-lies and workplaces, nurturing, tending, and empathizing are viewed as the natural talents that motivate female caregivers to help. Yet, like family and paid caregiving, the care women contribute to communities limits their access to resources of social power and privilege and thus contributes to gender inequality.

Gendered Division of Care Work

Women are more likely than men are to give care, informally, to friends and neighbors in their communities, and among the men and women who do care informally, women spend much more time at it.[10] Women are also more likely than men to give care formally, as volun-teers in organizations. Even though gender differences in rates of mem-bership in volunteer organizations are not great, women spend more time volunteering, and gender differences in volunteer time are greatest among those who volunteer most actively.[11] Men and women also do different kinds of work in voluntary organizations, with women doing more of the hands-on caregiving and men doing more in leadership and public relations. Robert Wuthnow's surveys of volunteers suggest that women are more involved in "activi-ties that are more nurturing, personal, and long-lasting" and that "women are also more likely to value [volunteer] nurturing and caring activities than men are."[12] Many people would explain these gendered patterns of care by women's natural dispositions. In this book, however, we have shown how women are channeled into nurturant and personal caregiving by exclusion from alternate activities and by positive encouragement. We also show how valuing care and doing it well develop from learning and practice rather than natural disposition: When women *do* more of the caregiving, they are more likely to understand care receivers' needs for care and more likely to value and feel invested in the caregiving that meets those needs.

Women continue to dominate time-consuming community caregiving, even now that nearly as many women as men are breadwinners. Schools, churches, and local charities still recruit women for volunteer caring work and do not often recruit men. Peer into elementary school classrooms or church kitchens and you will still see mostly mothers or female parishoners, some dressed in their work clothes, tutoring children or donning aprons to prepare the food. Teachers and ministers send the calls for help out to "mothers," as though their time is more available than fathers' time. And where these calls meet with too little success, disappointed organization members blame women's employment rather than employed fathers' lack of adaptation to new realities. Few PTA newsletters or church sermons refocus their moral appeals on persuading men to do more. They are more likely to rely on paid (female) staff than to work on spreading caregiving tasks more evenly between men and women.

Care Work and Social Resources

How does women's predominance in informal and hands-on community care affect gender inequality? The most direct link is that, like caregiving in the family, community help and voluntarism consumes time that might otherwise be invested in activities that confer wealth, power, and prestige. This applies particularly to informal helping, which can easily be as time-consuming, isolating, and invisible as family caregiving. Yet formal voluntarism can have similar effects. Some formal volunteer work improves access to resources like social recognition or advantageous contacts with people, but volunteers whose tasks are one-to-one, personal caregiving (most often women) will gain fewer of these resources of social power than those who attend meetings, disburse money, or meet the public.

Resources and Citizenship

A strength of community caregiving is its capacity to become a space for building a broader definition of citizenship. A woman's personal caregiving could become recognized as work that makes her a valued citizen. Yet, community caregiving in its gendered forms can also reinforce unequal citizenship. The different work men and women do in community groups builds different and unequal citizen capacities. When women specialize in *giving care* in communities and men specialize in *taking care of* others by coordinating voluntary effort or focusing on advocacy, women's care easily remains a less influential activity, inferior to more visible civic activity.

Men's community voluntarism—concentrating on leadership, organizational work, public relations, and advocacy—requires and develops skills in deliberation, persuasion, and administration and prepares volunteers for political citizenship. This kind of participation builds an individual's networks of civic deliberation and influence.[13]

Community caregivers who informally help neighbors or who volunteer for one-to-one parish outreach would benefit if we began to recognize how their caring work contributes to the common good. This would expand citizenship in the arena where women are most active.[14] Different citizenship is likely to remain unequal citizenship if different citizenship is associated with unequal access to power and privilege. Different citizenship reinforces other dynamics of gender inequality, as we elaborated in Chapter 5. If men and women are to become citizens who have equal respect, influence, and standing, women and men must share giving care and taking care of more equally.

Can Community Care Substitute for Government Support?

Americans' convictions about the advantages of community care, coupled with their mistrust of government-supported care, have led many people to advocate volunteer activity as a substitute for government programs. The examples that follow show how devolving responsibility for care from government to communities places insupportable burdens on communities and disproportionately burdens women— within families, in informal helping in communities, or in volunteer organizations. Our examples also show how intensifying women's care deepens inequalities beyond gender.

One striking example has been the deinstitutionalization of the mentally ill, which accelerated in the 1960s and continues today. The idea behind deinstitutionalization was to stop the "warehousing" of mentally ill people in large, state mental hospitals by returning them to community-based services and institutions. Hundreds of thousands of patients were released from commitment in hospitals and returned to communities that were ill-prepared to care for them.[15]

Scarce funding aborted the construction of enough community social services, group homes, and treatment centers to serve the deinstitutionalized population. Instead, many very ill people were returned to their families, where primary caregivers were mothers or wives. When families were unable to provide the extensive and specialized care mentally disabled family members needed, many families buckled and broke apart under the pressure of trying.[16] Former mental patients without families who would or could care for them swelled the ranks of homeless people, living in streets and shelters and receiving virtually no treatment or protection. Jails became the shelters of last resort, at huge public expense, but without therapeutic treatment. Deinstitutionalization presumed a capacity for community care that did not exist.[17]

A second example of devolution of care to communities that promises heavy burdens for women caregivers is the end of Aid to Families with Dependent Children (AFDC). As we described in the last chapter, the 1996 law that ended the federal welfare safety net responded to public concern that government-supported care, in the form of welfare, created damaging dependence and demoralized families.

The laws ending AFDC devolved responsibility for the poor to states and communities. Their proponents often asserted that help for the poor could best be designed and delivered in their own communities, with more of it provided by charities, rather than government. As we go to press, it is still too soon to know much about the effects of ending welfare. Yet, we might expect to see parallels to the deinstutionalization of the mentally ill—parallels involving many more families. If so, we should expect worse care for children and dependent elders and more care work for women.

Private charity has never produced levels of support comparable to recent government subsidies. Leaders of the charitable sector have agreed that voluntary effort cannot adequately substitute for government provision. Social scientists concur; an economist, for example, calculated that charitable contributions are likely to make up "no more than 35 cents, and perhaps less" of every dollar of government aid cut.[18] In states where the new law has been implemented fastest, more families live in homeless shelters, food pantries have been depleted and closed down, and churches that poor people attend have been inundated with requests for help with food, clothing, and shelter.[19]

Some commentators see "good news" in the fact that homelessness and requests to surrender children to foster care have not increased at the rate that critics of ending welfare predicted. The direst predictions about the end of welfare have not yet been confirmed. Yet, the deinstitutionalization experience suggests that we should look first at how families attempt to cope on their own. As yet, though, no one has counted how many single-mother families are now doubled up in housing with their relatives or how many have sent their children to live with relatives who can feed them. Doubling up and sending out children are strategies that rely primarily on women kin, and they impose great burdens upon them. These are the first solutions of families who become unable to make ends meet; when these fail, more visible problems spill into the communities.[20] Newspaper accounts in Milwaukee, Wisconsin, suggest families have begun employing such solutions: City landlords have recently coined a name, "W-2 stacks" (W-2 is the nickname of Wisconsin's post-welfare system), to describe apartments into which several poor families have crowded—a pattern they see increasing.[21]

There are other parallels with deinstitutionalizing mental illness that we might expect at welfare's end. When state mental health institutions shut their doors and communities failed to build the supports that former patients needed, social recognition of mental illness seemed to decline rather than sharpen. Although more sick people were on the streets or in neighborhoods, the decline in care discouraged people from "seeing" them. Perhaps it is too emotionally painful to perceive a person in need and not help. Whatever the reason, mentally ill people were increasingly "seen" as homeless men and women who need temporary shelter or as criminals who disturb the peace or harass or harm others, who need to be jailed. Studies estimate that between a quarter and half of the homeless are mentally ill. One follow-up of mentally ill patients discharged from an Ohio hospital found that 17 percent had been arrested within six months.[22]

A similar pattern could develop if families fail to thrive at welfare's end. Once communities fail to serve families' needs in the way they were able to do when welfare also subsidized families, they may similarly deflect the pain of failing to care. For example, overwhelmed charities may redefine who is "worthy" and restrict their help to those who find jobs and become low-income "breadwinners," excluding "irresponsible mothers" who do not find jobs or stay employed. Thus, single mothers who are crowded out of jobs by the glut of low-skilled workers required to find jobs may no longer be recognized in their communities or kinship networks as impoverished mothers of young children. Rather, communities may now "see" and treat them only as homeless people or as criminals who steal, sell sex, or commit child neglect.

Community care can complement government provision and support. In most instances, it will not be able to substitute for them. Voluntary care by women in family networks, neighborhoods, and community groups will not substitute for a government safety net for the very poor or very ill. Extreme and extensive need requires resources and coordination that are beyond the capabilities of communities. The case of deinstitutionalization and the plausible scenario we portray for the end of welfare suggest that the damaging consequences extend beyond harm done to those in need of care—to the integrity of communities and their shared norms of care.

Conclusion

Caregiving in communities has unique communal qualities and an "in-between-ness" that make it a distinctive kind of care in society. It can supplement some deficiencies in care provided by other institutions such as the family, the marketplace, or government. Communities are potentially important sites for collectively recognizing, revaluing, and expanding societywide commitment to caregiving. Communities also provide distinctive sites for pioneering responsive forms of care.

Yet, the resources in many communities are far too scarce to meet needs for caregiving. The appealing communal qualities of familiarity, trust, and we feeling can encourage exclusion and discrimination and also make care receiving more humiliating than it is in other sites of care. As well, a gendered division of labor in community volunteer work can significantly contribute to women's social disadvantage and inferior citizen status.

Just as the family cannot singly bear the responsibility of providing all the care that people in society need and want, and just as government policy cannot singly alter the gender inequalities associated with caregiving, communities cannot accomplish their distinctive contributions without the support of other social institutions. The concluding chapter will consider the ways in which action across institutions—linking the social sites of caregiving—might produce expanded, more responsive, and less gendered care.

CHAPTER 7

The Future of Caregiving

How will caregiving change in the twenty-first century United States? How do you think it should change? Some readers of this book probably agree with the authors that our society needs to value caregiving more highly and to provide more resources to support caring for children, for people who are ill and disabled, and for others in need. Some readers may also think that careqiving should be reorganized so that it no longer produces gender inequality.

From this point of view, many current trends in caregiving look discouraging, especially recent reductions in government support of caring and the very slow progress in men's sharing caregiving with women. Moving towards the twin goals of better care and gender equality may seem daunting, for it would require a major shift in the values and practices of individual citizens, as well as in the values of families, businesses, communities, and government policy makers.[1]

Other readers of this book are probably more content with current trends in caregiving, especially those who believe that it is natural and right for women to be the main caregivers. They may think that providing care is the responsibility of individual families and should not be a collective responsibility. These readers may see little need for change, other than the continued scaling back of government programs.

Throughout the book, although we have described views of caregiving that disagree with ours, we have marshaled our evidence to demonstrate that caregiving is gendered and that gendered care results in limited care and the subordination of women. In this concluding chapter, we review our major arguments about the social institutions that have produced gendered care and gender inequality. Then we suggest four social changes that could expand caregiving and gender equality in the future.

Explaining Gendered Caring
and Gender Inequality

Contemporary patterns of gendered caregiving in the United States have their roots in the nineteenth century ideology of "separate spheres" and the real separation of home and work that developed when men followed their work out of the home in industrial society. The institutions of home and work became gendered; only the home, and women within it, retained and refined the mission of tender caregiving.

Industrial workplaces envisioned workers as men whose home, children, and personal needs were tended at home by domestic caregivers. Work organizations could be places where caregiving need not be accommodated. When large-scale organizations developed to care for those who could not be cared for in families, employers saw paid caregivers as bringing domestic, natural, female caring into the workplace. Caregiving skills remained unrecognized and poorly rewarded. Nurses, teachers, social workers, and their untrained counterparts were paid far less than male workers of comparable skill.

Political forces also shaped caregiving. When European countries began to build welfare states that offered government support of family care, the United States resisted policies of "big government." No powerful labor party coalitions championed an ample social safety net, as they did in parts of Europe. Corporate interests more effectively resisted regulation and taxation to expand government's role in care. When the United States finally built a welfare system, it emphasized moderate but dignified benefits for workers and their dependents. Caregiving itself earned little entitlement: only a meager and stigmatizing program of welfare for poor single mothers. Earning, not caring, became the mark of citizens worthy of government's benefits.

Embedded in our social institutions, these patterns continue to influence caregiving. Women are still expected to care, both in the family and in the workplace. Caregiving is socially valued in some ways, but because women, primarily, are the caregivers, whoever gives care pays a considerable price in social power, privilege, and prestige.

Women's caregiving lowers their income, power, status, and choices in ways we have discussed throughout this book. Women caregivers often curtail their education or their work to care for their families. As a result, they lose income relative to men and may well become poor, especially in the United States, which lacks government programs to offset caregivers' loss of income and pension benefits and job advancement when they interrupt work. Professional women (and men) with major caregiving responsibilities find they cannot fit into a career pattern that is designed for men and requires successful workers to work full-time or more, without interruptions for family caregiving. Women also lack the support of a "wife" or devoted partner that many successful men enjoy.

As a result of these processes, women earn less money than men. The differences in income and earning potential between women and men contributes to the marital power of husbands over wives. Husbands use this power to avoid caregiving; they delegate to wives the kinds of time-consuming care that interferes with investing time and energy in work and reaping its benefits.

The gendered organization of caregiving not only subordinates women, it also subordinates and devalues caring. Partly because caring is seen as an instinctual ability of women, the skill and knowledge required for good caregiving remain generally unrecognized and underpaid, especially skills related to the interpersonal or emotional aspects of caring, which are seen as built-in "feminine" traits.

These skills were ignored in the ways caregiving was conceived in the job descriptions, pay scales, and authority lines of early forms of caring work, like nursing. Caregiving organizations took shape without the need to hire skilled caregivers or to train and certify them. Their administrators were free to engage in competitive cost cutting, holding down labor costs by defining most caregiving work as unskilled. Professional caregivers, like hospital doctors, could define caregiving skills narrowly, in their own image, like the medical model of care does.

The devaluation of care thus became institutionalized, and it persists in the routine roles and practices that contemporary organizations inherited and repeat. Whether in hospitals, social service agencies, or nursing homes, managers and professionals (predominantly European American and male) retain authority, high wages, and social respect. Hands-on caregivers (predominantly female, immigrants, and people of color) continue to have little authority and to earn rock-bottom wages and little social respect. Embedded in social institutions, the devaluation of caregiving and the low wages of caregivers have become taken-for-granted "facts of life."

So the devaluation of care and the subordination of women are linked social processes. Could they be unlinked? Could women become equal to men without diminishing caregiving? Could the United States provide more caregiving while moving toward gender equality? Our final section outlines some preliminary answers to these questions.

Paths to Expanding Care and Gender Equality

Four groups of changes, together, could both expand caregiving and make it more gender equal. The first set of changes involves building a widespread consensus on the value of care as well as a collective commitment to better care and gender equity. The second set aims to develop institutions of social care that support and complement caregiving in families. The third set rewards caregiving on the same level as other valued work and other duties of citizenship. The fourth set of changes involves creating gender equality in both opportunities and obligations to care.

1. Build Recognition of the Value of Caregiving and a Collective Commitment to Better Care

Every Mother's Day, and with every news account of child or elder neglect, we acknowledge the value of good caregiving. In between those events, many Americans seem to take caregiving for granted. Yet, it has become more difficult than ever to take caregiving for granted. New ideas about men's and women's roles raise questions in every arena about who should be doing what. At a time when parents grieve over too little time to spend with children, and when the normal problems of sickness and aging threaten to disrupt and impoverish families, many Americans may be ready to initiate a national discussion about the value of better care; they may be ready to make the political and economic commitments that are needed to achieve it.

The United States has changed values and priorities before, through the efforts of government leaders, the media, unions, business, and other groups of citizens. These groups debated and participated in major social projects, such as creating free public education and fighting World War II and the "War on Poverty."[2] Like these national initiatives, an initiative on caregiving will require not only recognizing its value, but facing up to the difficult mission of achieving it.[3]

Revaluing and expanding caregiving is difficult both because it requires considerable deliberation and political commitment and because it entails costs that citizens must be willing to pay. To produce solid change, deliberation about caregiving would have to take place at many levels of society. Discussions among caregivers and care receivers in local communities could link with local, state, and national efforts to assess needs for care and develop solutions.

Grassroots political organizing could be an important part of building a commitment to improved caregiving and gender equality. Many effective groups that lobby for better caregiving have already been formed by the families of children or adults with particular needs for care. For example, in some communities, caregivers of the elderly have organized to obtain better services for both care receivers and caregivers. Women Who Care, founded in Marin County, California in 1977, began as a support group for wives caring for disabled husbands. As the women exchanged stories about their problems with finding adequate services, they recognized the need to take political action. The group developed programs of respite care, home care, and community education. They also launched a national campaign of education and publicity about the needs of caregivers in cooperation with the Older Women's League (the slogan of OWL is "Don't agonize—organize"). Other nationwide or community groups focus on caring for young children, disabled people, or people with specific diseases such as Alzheimer's disease, stroke, or cancer.[4] Still others champion equitable wages for child care workers or nursing assistants. Creating a coalition of these issue-specific groups will be a major challenge and a first step toward constructing a national caregiving agenda that includes all citizens.

Persuading Americans to accept the economic and social costs of expanding caregiving and gender equity will also be challenging. Achieving better care, even better unpaid care, will be expensive. It requires policies, such as paid leaves, that enable paid workers to be caregivers. The costs of paid leaves must be paid by businesses or by government funds provided by taxpayers.

In European countries, businesses are willing to contribute to paid leaves because popular policies require it. Business does not pay most of the cost of social care in these countries, however—government substantially subsidizes care and provides caregiving services. This requires the higher taxes that European countries levy and that their corporations and individual citizens accept in exchange for a safety net of social care. Americans have agreed to pay higher taxes in the past for the goal of waging war; we could agree to pay higher taxes to expand caregiving.

Expanding caregiving would entail other financial costs as well. To provide adequate rewards to paid caregivers, employers would have to raise their pay, grant them standard work benefits such as health care and pensions, and give them opportunities for further training and job advancement. These improvements would raise the costs of nursing homes and day care and reduce profits for these businesses. If the improvements were subsidized by the government, it would raise taxes.

A fair program for rewarding caregivers might share the costs of caring among all citizens. Citizens in the United States and elsewhere have been most supportive of sharing the costs of care when the benefits are available to everyone. This might mean the kind of universal child care benefits that France offers (as we discussed in Chapter 5).

Expanding caregiving would require new commitments that modify longstanding beliefs and priorities of many Americans. Public opinion and government policy would have to place greater emphasis on collective responsibility for taking care of others and place less emphasis on free enterprise, individualism, and self-sufficient families. This means making caregiving a citizen's duty as well a national goal. New commitment to the virtues and tasks of caregiving might temper older beliefs about the dangers of big government. To allow families the time they need to care, and to enable paid caregivers to do better caregiving, voters would have to be willing to regulate profit making so as to improve caring.

Inducing men to shoulder their fair share of the work of caring will be especially challenging. Many of the costs of moving toward gender equity in caregiving would fall upon men, who are now often exempt from the obligations of caregiving. We discuss this element of a national commitment to caregiving in item 4.

Enacting a national agenda on caring would require the active participation of many individuals and groups, ranging from families to grassroots organizations to big business and state and federal governments. A national commitment to adequate care for all citizens would be a major shift in American society, but dedicated Americans have created such shifts before.

2. Support and Complement Family Caregiving With a System of Social Care

The United States lags way behind other affluent nations in its provisions of "social care," or funds and services from government, business, and community organizations to complement family caregiving. Social care has a long history in the United States, however, from our earliest forms of local charity to the early federal Children's Bureau to the massive network of voluntary community groups to Social Security and Medicare.

The U.S. government at the state and federal level is more involved in caregiving than many people realize. For example, 70 percent of the states already give some form of cash payment or vouchers to families caring for someone who is mentally or physically disabled. Families can use funds or a voucher to pay for a homeworker or attendant. On the federal level, the Department of Veterans Affairs' Universal Aid and Attendance Allowance gives unrestricted direct cash payments to 220,000 disabled veterans.[5] Although these state and federal programs are small, they show that some government support of caregiving is already widely accepted in the United States.

In the business community, firms are increasingly providing services for caregivers through flextime, child care support, flexible benefits, and other programs. These programs are still unusual, and they are typically restricted to higher level professional employees.[6] However, some exceptional companies offer models that other companies might be persuaded to follow, with enough pressure from public opinion and government policies. Bristol-Meyers Squibb Company, for example, extends its family leave policy to all full-time and part-time employees who have worked for one year for at least 1,000 hours (although temporary workers are excluded). Nonetheless, most companies resist extending supports for caregiving because they are expensive.[7]

Critics of social care argue that government support for caring could make family caregiving more voluntary and less enforceable. In Chapter 5, we agreed that this may be true, but we also showed how social care can complement and enrich family care and can provide for those who are not well cared for in families. For these reasons, social care is an important consideration for a national care initiative.

A coordinated system of social care appears to be a necessary element of gender equality, as well. In the United States and other countries, support and services outside the family have helped women combine earning and caring. They have also enabled women to become less dependent on marriage for their family's survival. Social care by itself does not necessarily produce gender equality, as we saw in the case of Sweden; it seems to be a necessary but not sufficient step toward gender equality and gender-equal care.

3. *Reward Paid and Unpaid Caregiving on the Same Level as Other Productive Work and Other Duties of Citizenship*

Housewives, day care workers, and nurses' aides typically receive little respect, income, pensions, or other benefits and do very difficult work with inadequate resources of time, money, and supportive services. One reason that men avoid caregiving and many women choose other options when they are available is that caregiving brings so few external rewards and entails so many personal costs. To implement a national commitment to better caregiving, Americans would have to take account of the effort and skills involved in good caregiving. Then we could accord caregivers the respect and rewards appropriate to their contributions.

The effort, learning, and skill that go into good care has long been invisible. Caregiving knowledge is largely unwritten and unsystematized. Learning takes place in unacknowledged "apprenticeships" in the family and on the job, and skill is misinterpreted as an expression of the inner nature of the caregiver.

To take account of the work of caregiving, we must begin to distil its knowledge, require and reward learning it, and recognize and reward the effort and skill caregivers use. The profession of nursing has struggled, with some success, to accomplish that. Child care workers, who currently are paid less than janitors, will not be adequately appreciated and compensated until we recognize that to do a good job, they need to learn complex procedures and bodies of knowledge, in both formal educational programs and on-the-job training that apprentices them to master caregivers. The U.S. Army's Child Care program, described in Chapter 5, rewards good caregivers who study and demonstrate competence in skills by promoting them to higher positions with better pay and more authority.

Taking account of the skill and knowledge used by caregivers in the family is also possible. Many Americans already value family caregiving highly. They believe that raising a child is demanding and requires many complex interpersonal and emotional skills. Yet, viewing skills as natural to mothers, many are still reluctant to give domestic caregivers the supports and rewards that paid workers receive. Under current policies, unpaid caregivers are not entitled to the rewards of citizenship that are primarily available to breadwinners. They are entitled to citizen benefits only as "dependents" of breadwinners. We could, however, use citizen entitlements to recognize the social contribution of unpaid caregivers—in families or in community voluntary associations.[8]

Time spent caring for a newborn or a sick elder could be considered work that counts toward an old age pension; it could be paid a wage or income supplement; it could be covered by health or disability insurance and followed by unemployment insurance or job retraining. It could entitle a woman or man to respite services or time off from care. Examples of each of these entitlements for caregivers abound in European welfare systems and in U.S. pilot programs. They are costly, of course, but we could decide that good care is worth it.[9]

4. Create Gender Equality in Opportunities and Obligations to Care

Even if caregiving were better recognized and rewarded, if it remains women's domain, women and men will not become social equals. A national initiative on caregiving could begin to "ungender" the meanings and images of caregiving. It could encourage men to be caregivers. It could empower women to negotiate more involvement in caregiving with male partners. It could increase the costs of evasion to parents and citizens who are obliged to care.

Anyone who imagines the impossibility of altering old ideas about women and caregiving is forgetting that in a few recent decades other old, entrenched ideas about men and women have all but disappeared among younger generations and have faded even among older ones. Contemporary advertising shows us numerous images of men as tender and empathic fathers, as advertisers cannily appeal to our deep longings. The messages about men and care we increasingly hear from the pulpit nowadays emphasize men's as well as women's moral commitments to care. Ideals have already begun to change; a concerted effort could accelerate it.

Throughout this book, we have shown how the actions of families, communities, employers, and governments channel women to focus on caregiving and men to focus on breadwinning. Gender equity requires major changes in all these institutions. Families could teach and model the value of caregiving for both genders. They could teach boys and girls to babysit and to play competitive sports. Children could learn at home that caring for others is part of being a respected person, a "real man" or a "real woman."[10]

Employers could lure men into caregiving jobs by equalizing wages between jobs that are female dominated and those that are male dominated, if they are of comparable effort and skill. Specifically taking account of the skills in caregiving, they could raise the wages and increase the autonomy of paid caregivers. They could restructure jobs so that it becomes easier to combine a successful career with major caregiving responsibilities. They could prove that parental leaves and other family-friendly policies are meant to be used by men as well as women, by promoting those who use them. They could ask managers themselves to take parental and sick care leave.

Gender-equalizing measures threaten higher labor costs for business, so it may take government action to enforce fair employment practices. The U.S. government has a history of promoting fairness in the workplace, justifying policies on moral grounds, not on the basis of profit. Although we have done less in this area than most other countries, a national debate about "family-friendly policies" is well under way here. This debate might be enriched and accelerated if it were linked with a broader care initiative.

Throughout the book, we suggest a number of ways that government could make caregiving more gender equal. Policies that recognize and reward paid and unpaid caregiving, such as comparable worth wage policies or parental leaves, encourage men to give care, and they undercut the disadvantages of employed female caregivers. Policies that curb the demands of the workplace in ways that give all workers more time for family encourage men and women to share the tasks of earning and caring.

In addition to encouraging men to give care, government policies can also empower women to bargain individually with their partners for a fairer division of caregiving at home. In general, laws and policies that increase women's social status and resources empower women to make effective demands on men's domestic labor. We showed in Chapter 3 how wives' employment and income enable them to bargain for more domestic work from husbands. Thus, employment policies that are not directly related to caregiving may be especially important supports for getting men to share the work of caregiving at home. Similarly, policies that support single-mother families make the possibility of living independently a bargaining resource for wives. Policies that shorten the work day would also make it easier for women to negotiate a shift of men's attention from work to caregiving.

In addition to supporting and providing social care, making caregiving more appealing to men, and empowering women to make better domestic bargains over care, government can also make care a valued duty of citizenship and increase the individual costs of evading care. If our deliberations about caregiving led us to view caregiving as a social contribution similar to breadwinning, law and policy could sanction the failure to care.

Old age pensions and other social insurance could reward the sacrifice of giving care in families or communities, as well the sacrifices of breadwinning for others or military service. Divorce and child custody decisions could take account of the life-long costs of intensive care of children and assure that noncaregiving parents share the costs fairly. Policies that subsidize and create services of care would represent the duty of all citizens to contribute to care. These policies establish the citizenship duties of care and sanction those who fail their obligations.[11]

Could we make our society more caring and still move toward gender equality? We think we could, and it must be apparent that we believe we should. This chapter suggests that the task is complex and difficult but possible. This book, we hope, has presented some knowledge and concepts that will be useful in understanding the complexity of caring and gender and thinking strategically about paths of change.

Notes and References

Chapter 1

1. Our approach to defining caregiving draws heavily on Finch, Janet, and Dulcie Groves, eds. 1983. *A Labour of Love: Women, Work and Caring*. London: Routledge and Kegan Paul, especially Hilary Graham's essay, "Caring: A Labour of Love," pp. 13-30, and Clare Ungerson's essay, "Why Do Women Care?" pp. 31-50. Also see Ungerson, Clare. 1990. "The Language of Care: Crossing the Boundaries." Pp. 8-33 in *Gender and Caring: Work and Welfare in Britain and Scandinavia*, edited by Clare Ungerson. New York: Harvester Wheatsheaf.

2. In the field of feminist ethics, several authors have proposed a precise definition of caring that includes diversity by emphasizing responsiveness to the care receiver. See especially Noddings, Nel. 1984. *Caring: A Feminine Approach to Ethics and Moral Education*. Berkeley: University of California Press; Ruddick, Sara. 1989. *Maternal Thinking: Toward a Politics of Peace*. Boston: Beacon.

3. On the importance of power in caring relationships, see Ungerson, 1990, op. cit.

4. For excellent surveys of feminist perspectives on caregiving from a sociological perspective, see Abel, Emily K., and Margaret K. Nelson. 1990. *Circles of Care*. Albany: State University of New York Press; Finch and Groves, 1983, op. cit.; and Hooyman, Nancy R., and Judith Gonyea. 1995. *Feminist Perspectives on Family Care*. Newbury Park, CA: Sage.

5. Cancian, Francesca. 1986. "The Feminization of Love." *Signs* 11:692-709.

6. Lorber, Judith. 1993. "Believing Is Seeing: Biology as Ideology." *Gender & Society* 7:568-81.

7. The concept of *social institutions* is explained in Berger, Peter L. and Thomas Luckmann. 1980. *The Social Construction of Reality*. New York: Irvington; also, Turner, Jonathan. 1997. *The Institutional Order*. New York: Longman.

8. Lopata, Helena. 1993. "The Interweave of Public and Private: Women's Challenge to American Society." *Journal of Marriage and the Family* 55:176-90.

9. For feminist perspectives on family caring, see Marx Feree, Myra. 1990. "Beyond Separate Spheres: Feminism and Family Research." *Journal of Marriage and the Family* 52:866-84; also, Thompson, Linda. 1992.

"Feminist Methodology for Family Studies." *Journal of Marriage and the Family* 54:3-18.

10. Abel, Emily K., and Margaret K. Nelson. 1990. "Circles of Care: Introductory Essay." Pp. 4-34 in *Circles of Care*, edited by Emily K. Abel and Margaret K. Nelson. Albany: State University of New York Press.

11. Tronto, Joan C. 1993. *Moral Boundaries: A Political Argument for an Ethic of Care.* New York: Routledge.

12. For an empirical study of how social inequalities interact with paid caregiving, see Sacks, Karen. 1988. *Caring by the Hour: Women, Work and Organizing at Duke Medical Center.* Urbana: University of Illinois Press.

13. For an excellent example of how race and social status shape standards of good care in a preschool, see Lubeck, Sally. 1985. *Sandbox Society: Early Education in Black and White America.* London: Falmer.

Chapter 2

1. Demos, John. 1970. *A Little Commonwealth.* London: Oxford University Press.

2. Demos, John. 1986. *Past, Present, and Personal.* New York: Oxford University Press, p. 28; Ulrich, Laurel Thatcher. 1982. *Good Wives.* New York: Knopf.

3. Ulrich, 1982, op. cit.

4. Demos, 1986, op. cit.; Greven, Philip. 1977. *The Protestant Temperament.* New York: Knopf; Ulrich, 1982, op. cit.

5. Greven, 1977, op. cit., pp. 34, 35.

6. Ibid., p. 23.

7. Ibid.

8. Pollock, Linda A. 1983. *Forgotten Children.* Cambridge, UK: Cambridge University Press.

9. Ryan, Mary P. 1983. *Womanhood in America from Colonial Times to the Present.* 3d ed. New York: Watts; Ulrich, 1982, op. cit.

10. Ulrich, 1982, op. cit., pp. 157-58.

11. Ryan, 1983, op. cit.

12. Greven, 1977, op. cit., pp. 31, 36, 159, 168.

13. Ibid., p. 38.

14. Ibid.

15. Demos, 1986, op. cit.

16. Ibid.

17. Ibid.

18. Ibid., p. 48.

19. Coontz, Stephanie. 1988. *The Social Origins of Private Life*. London: Verso, p. 56.

20. Ibid.; Demos, John. 1994. *The Unredeemed Captive*. New York: Knopf.

21. Demos, 1994, op. cit., p. 144.

22. Coontz, 1988, op. cit.

23. Demos, 1994, op. cit., p. 142.

24. Ibid.

25. Jones, Jacqueline. 1985. *Labor of Love, Labor of Sorrow*. New York: Vintage; Gutman, Herbert G. 1976. *The Black Family in Slavery and Freedom, 1750-1925*. New York: Pantheon.

26. Jones, 1985, op. cit.; Gutman, 1976, op. cit.

27. Genovese, Eugene D. 1974. *Roll, Jordan, Roll*. New York: Pantheon.

28. Jones, 1985, op. cit.

29. Ibid.

30. Gutman, 1976, op. cit.

31. Jones, 1985, op. cit., p. 29.

32. Boydston, Jeanne. 1990. *Home and Work: Housework, Wages, and the Ideology of Labor in the Early Republic*. New York: Oxford University Press.

33. Ibid.

34. Ryan, 1983, op. cit.; Rotundo, E. Anthony. 1993. *American Manhood*. New York: Basic Books.

35. Rotundo, 1993, op. cit.

36. Boydston, Jeanne. 1990. *Home and Work: Housework*. New York: Oxford University Press.

37. Ibid.

38. Ibid., p. 163.

39. Ryan, 1983, op cit.; Cott Nancy F. 1977. *The Bonds of Womanhood*. New Haven, CT: Yale University Press.

40. Boydston, 1990, op. cit.

41. Cott, 1977, op. cit., p. 88.

42. Boydston, 1990, op. cit.

43. Cott, 1977, op. cit.

44. Welter, Barbara. 1978. "The Cult of True Womanhood: 1820-1860." Pp. 224-50 in *The American Family in Social-Historical Perspective*, edited by Michael Gordon. New York: St. Martin's.

45. Boydston, 1990, op. cit.

46. Ibid., p. 143.

47. Coontz, 1988, op. cit., p. 210.

48. Gordon, Linda. 1988. *Heroes of Their Own Lives: The Politics and History of Family Violence.* New York: Viking Penguin.

49. Ibid.

50. Ryan, 1983, op. cit.

51. Zelizer, Viviana. 1985. *Pricing the Priceless Child.* New York: Basic Books.

52. Jones, 1985, op. cit.; Peiss, Kathy. 1986. *Cheap Amusement.* Philadelphia: Temple University Press.

53. Acker, Joan. 1990. "Hierarchies, Jobs, Bodies: A Theory of Gendered Organizations." *Gender & Society* 4:139-58.

54. Berg, Barbara J. 1978. *The Remembered Gate.* Oxford: Oxford University Press.

55. Ibid.

56. Reverby, Susan. 1990. "The Duty or Right to Care." Pp. 132-49 in *Circles of Care: Work and Identity in Women's Lives,* edited by Emily K. Abel and Margaret K. Nelson. Albany, NY: State University of New York Press.

57. Bullough, Vern L., and Bonnie Bullough. 1969. *The Emergence of Modern Nursing.* London: MacMillan.

58. Ibid.; Melosh, Barbara. 1982. *The Physician's Hand.* Philadelphia: Temple University Press.

59. Reverby, Susan. 1987. *Ordered to Care: The Dilemma of American Nursing.* New York: Cambridge University Press.

60. Ibid.; Bullough and Bullough, 1969, op. cit.

61. Reverby, 1987, op. cit.

62. Ibid.; Kalisch, Philip A., and Beatrice J. Kalisch. 1995. *The Advance of American Nursing.* 3d ed. Philadelphia: Lippincott.

63. Reverby, 1987, op. cit.

64. Ibid.; Bullough and Bullough, 1969, op. cit.

65. Reverby, 1987, op. cit.

66. Abbott, Andrew. 1988. *The System of the Professions.* Chicago: University of Chicago Press.

67. Starr, Paul. 1982. *The Social Transformation of American Medicine.* New York: Basic Books; Melosh, Barbara. 1982. *The Physician's Hand.* Philadelphia: Temple University Press.

68. Ashley, Jo Anne. 1976. *Hospitals, Paternalism, and the Role of the Nurse.* New York: Teachers College Press, p. 80.

69. Ibid., p. 77.

70. Abbott, 1988, op. cit.

71. Reverby, 1987, op. cit.; Abbott, 1988, op. cit.

72. Abbott, 1988, op. cit.

73. Reverby, 1987, op. cit.; Melosh, 1982, op. cit.

74. Ibid.; Kalisch and Kalisch, 1995, op. cit.

75. Melosh, 1982, op. cit.

76. Ibid.

77. Ibid.

78. Ibid.; Kalisch and Kalisch, 1995, op. cit.

79. Brannon, Robert. 1994. *Intensifying Care*. Amityville, NY: Baywood.

80. Tyack, David B., and Myra Strober. 1981. "Jobs and Gender." Pp. 131-52 in *Education Policy and Management*, edited by Patricia A. Schmuck, W. W. Charters, Jr., and Richard O. Carlson. New York: Academic; Trattner, Walter T. 1994. *From Poor Law to Welfare State*. 5th ed. New York: Free Press; Etzioni, Amitai, ed. 1969. *The Semi-Professions and Their Organization*. New York: Free Press.

Chapter 3

1. Yankelovich, Daniel. 1981. *New Rules*. New York: Random House, p. 93.

2. Brownstein, Robert. 1995. "Discontent Threatens Both Parties as U. S. '96 Vote Nears." *Los Angeles Times*, November 5, pp. A21, A20.

3. Hayge, Howard. [1990]. "Family Members in the Work Force." *Monthly Labor Review* 113(3):14-19; U.S. Bureau of the Census. 1997. *Employment Characteristics of Families Summary*. Washington, DC: U.S. Government Printing Office. Retrieved [May 5, 1998] from the World Wide Web: http://stats.bls.gov/news.release/famee.t02.htm

4. U.S. Bureau of the Census. 1997. *Statistical Abstract of the United States*. Washington, DC: U.S. Government Printing Office, p. 404.

5. Coltrane, Scott. 1989. "Household Labor and the Routine Production of Gender. *Social Problems* 36:473-90.

6. The data on children in single parent families are from Bumpass, Larry L., and R. Kelly Raley. 1995. "Redefining Single-Parent Families: Cohabitation and Changing Family Reality." *Demography* 32:97-115. The poverty data are from the U.S. Bureau of the Census. 1998. *Current Population Survey*. Washington, DC: U.S. Government Printing Office.

7. Kurz, Demie. 1995. *For Richer, For Poorer: Mothers Confront Divorce*. New York: Routledge. The child support data are from p. 7.

8. Ibid., pp. 7-8.

9. For details on how these unpublished interviews were conducted, see Cancian, Francesca. 1987. *Love in America: Gender and Self-Development*.

New York: Cambridge University Press. Catherine Rowley was a student in my seminar on interviewing families. She assigned the "Blaines" fictitious first and last names to protect their anonymity. Fictitious names were used for all cases in this study.

10. Pyke, Karen D. 1996. "Class-based Masculinities: The Interdependence of Gender, Class, and Interpersonal Power." *Gender & Society* 10:527-49; Rubin, Lillian B. 1976. *Worlds of Pain: Life in the Working Class Family.* New York: Basic Books.

11. Glenn, Evelyn Nakano. 1992. "From Servitude to Service Work: Historical Continuities in the Racial Division of Women's Work." *Signs* 18:1-43.

12. U.S. Bureau of the Census, 1997, op. cit., p. 78.

13. For the employment rate of mothers, see U.S. Department of Labor Statistics, Labor Force Statistics From the Current Population Survey "Employment Characteristics of Families Summary." Retrieved February 20, 1999 from the World Wide Web: http://stats.bls.gov/newreels.htm The data on child care are from the U.S. Bureau of the Census, http://www.census.gov/population/socdemo/child, May 21, 1998.

14. Clarke-Stewart, Alison. 1993. *Daycare.* Rev. ed. Cambridge, MA: Harvard University Press.

15. U.S. Bureau of the Census. 1997. "C1. Percent of Children Under 5 in Selected Child Care Arrangements: 1997-1993." Retrieved November 21, 1997 from the World Wide Web: http://www.census.gov/population/socdemo/child.cctab1.txt

16. Ibid.

17. Ibid., pp. 131.

18. Ibid., pp. 18 and 23.

19. Robinson, John P., and Geoffrey Godbey. 1997. *Time for Life: The Surprising Ways Americans Use Their Time.* University Park, PA: Pennsylvania State University Press.

20. Bergmann, Barbara R. 1996. *Saving Our Children From Poverty: What the United States Can Learn From France.* New York: Russell Sage Foundation.

21. Coltrane, Scott. 1988. "Father-Child Relationships and the Status of Women: A Cross-Cultural Study." *American Journal of Sociology* 93:1060-95.

22. On family violence and abuse, see Gelles, Richard. 1994. "Family Violence, Abuse, and Neglect." Pp. 262-80 in *Families and Change: Coping with Stressful Events,* edited by Patrick C. McKenry and Sharon J. Price. Newbury Park, CA: Sage. Estimates on childlessness are from Morgan, Philip S., and Renbao Chen. 1992. "Predicting Childlessness for Recent Cohorts of American Women." *International Journal of Forecasting* 8:477-93.

23. Thompson, Linda, and Alexis J. Walker. 1989. "Gender in Families: Women and Men in Marriage, Work and Parenthood." *Journal of Marriage and Family* 51:845-71.

24. McMahon, Martha. 1995. *Engendering Motherhood: Identity and Self-Transformation in Women's Lives.* New York: Guilford, p. 163.

25. Ibid., pp. 175-76.

26. Coltrane, Scott. 1996. *Family Man: Fatherhood, Housework, and Gender Equity.* New York: Oxford University Press; Gerson, Kathleen. 1993. *No Man's Land: Men's Changing Commitments to Family and Work.* New York: Basic Books. The data on divorced fathers are from Seltzer, Judith A. 1991. "Relationships between Fathers and Children Who Live Apart." *Journal of Marriage and the Family* 53:79-101.

27. Frodi, A. M., M. E. Lamb, L. A. Leavitt, and W. L. Donovan. 1978. "Fathers' and Mothers' Responses to Infant Smiles and Cries." *Infant Behavior and Development* 1:187-98.

28. Parke, Ross D. 1981. *Fathers.* Cambridge, MA: Harvard University Press, p. 28.

29. Coltrane, 1989, op. cit., pp. 475-76.

30. Parke, 1981, op. cit.

31. The data on fathers' family work are from Acock, Alan C., and David H. Demo. 1994. *Family Diversity and Well-Being.* Newbury Park, CA: Sage. Also see Robinson and Godbey, 1997, op. cit., and Coltrane, 1996, op. cit.

32. Vannoy-Hiller, Dana, and William W. Philliber. 1989. *Equal Partners: Successful Women's Marriages.* Newbury Park, CA: Sage.

33. Chodorow, Nancy. 1978. *The Reproduction of Mothering.* Berkeley: University of California Press.

34. Connell, R. W. 1995. *Masculinities.* Berkeley: University of California Press.

35. Traustadottir, Rannveig. 1997. "Disability Reform and Women's Caring Work." Presented at the Conference on Gender, Citizenship and the Work of Caring, November 14-16, University of Illinois at Urbana-Champaign.

36. West, Candace, and Don Zimmerman. 1987. "Doing Gender." *Gender & Society* 1:125-51.

37. Traustadottir, 1997, op. cit.

38. Machung, Anne. 1989. "Talking Career, Thinking Job: Gender Differences in Career and Family Expectations of Berkeley Seniors." *Feminist Studies* 15:35-58.

39. Ibid., p. 51.

40. Collins, Randall, and Scott Coltrane. 1995. *Sociology of Marriage and the Family.* 3d ed. Chicago: Nelson-Hall.

41. Blood, Robert O., and Donald M. Wolfe. 1960. *Husbands and Wives: The Dynamics of Married Living*. New York: Free Press. See also MacDonald, G. W. 1980. "Family Power: The Assessment of a Decade of Theory and Research." *Journal of Marriage and the Family* 42:840-54, and Pyke, Karen D. 1994. "Women's Employment as a Gift or a Burden? Marital Power Across Marriage, Divorce and Remarriage." *Gender & Society* 8:73-91.

42. Reskin, Barbara, and Irene Padavic. 1994. *Women and Men at Work*. Thousand Oaks, CA: Pine Forge Press.

43. Coltrane, 1996, op. cit.

44. Gerson, Kathleen. 1985. *Hard Choices: How Women Decide About Work, Career and Motherhood*. Berkeley: University of California Press, p. 87.

45. Cancian, 1987, op. cit.; Oliker, Stacey. 1989. *Best Friends and Marriage: Exchange Among Women*. Berkeley: University of California Press.

46. Blumstein, Philip, and Pepper Schwartz. 1983. *American Couples*. New York: Longman, p. 519.

47. Ibid., pp. 453-54.

48. Ibid., pp. 334-35.

49. Cancian, 1987, op. cit.

50. Hochschild, Arlie. 1975. "Inside the Clockwork of a Male Career." Pp. 47-80 in *Women and the Power to Change*, edited by Florence Howe. New York: McGraw-Hill; Pyke, 1996, op. cit.

51. Gleason, Holly. 1995. "Corporate Executives' Wives: The Privileged Lonely?" Sociology Honors Thesis, Department of Sociology, University of California, Irvine. On marriages of the very wealthy, see Ostrander, Susan. 1984. *Women of the Upper Class*. Philadelphia: Temple University Press.

52. Gleason, 1995, op. cit., p. 7.

53. Ibid., p. 6.

54. Ibid., p. 6.

55. Ibid., p. 6.

56. Cancian, 1987, op. cit., pp. 91-102. The quote from Mornell is on page 91. Also see Thompson, Linda. 1993. "Conceptualizing Gender in Marriage: The Case of Marital Care." *Journal of Marriage and the Family* 55:557-69.

57. Rubin, Lillian B. 1976. *Worlds of Pain: Life in the Working Class Family*. New York: Basic Books, pp. 120-21.

58. Hochschild, Arlie. 1989. *The Second Shift: Working Parents and the Revolution at Home*. New York: Viking.

59. U.S. Bureau of the Census, 1998, *Current Population Survey*, op. cit.

60. Hymowitz, Carol. 1997. "Lost in the Rush." *Wall Street Journal*, March 31, p. 1 of special section, "Work and the Family."

61. Oliker, Stacey J. 1995. "The Proximate Contexts of Workfare and Work: A Framework for Studying Poor Women's Economic Choices." *The Sociological Quarterly* 36:251-72.

62. Robinson and Godbey, 1997, op. cit.

63. Leira, Arnlaug. 1997. "Caring and Social Rights: What Does 'Daddy Leave' Entail?" Presented at the Conference on Gender, Citizenship and the Work of Caring, November 14-16, University of Illinois at Urbana-Champaign.

64. Gauthier, Anne Helene. 1996. *The State and the Family: A Comparative Analysis of Family Policies in Industrialized Countries.* Oxford: Clarendon.

65. Hooyman, Nancy, and Judith Gonyea. 1995. *Feminist Perspectives on Family Care.* Newbury Park, CA: Sage.

66. Treas, Judith. 1995. "Older Americans in the 1990s and Beyond." *Population Bulletin* 50(2):1-46.

67. Ibid., p. 6.

68. Glazer, Nona. 1993. *Women's Paid and Unpaid Labor.* Philadelphia: Temple University Press.

69. Treas, 1995, op. cit., p. 33.

70. Stone, Robyn, Gail Lee Cafferata, and Judith Sangl. 1987. "Caregivers of the Frail Elderly: A National Profile." *The Gerontologist* 27:616-26.

71. Ibid.

72. Abel, Emily K. 1991. *Who Cares For The Elderly?* Philadelphia: Temple University Press, p. 77.

73. Ibid.

74. Baldwin, Sally, and Caroline Glendinning. 1983. "Employment, Women, and Their Disabled Children." Pp. 53-71 in *A Labour of Love: Women, Work, and Caring,* edited by Janet Finch and Dulcie Groves. London: Routledge and Kegan Paul.

75. Abel, 1991, op. cit., p. 67.

76. Ibid., p. 68.

77. Treas, 1995, op. cit.

78. Abel, 1991, op. cit.; Horowitz, A. 1985. "Family Caregivinq to the Frail Elderly." *Annual Review of Gerontology and Geriatrics* 5:194-246; Oliver, Judith. 1983. "The Caring Wife." Pp. 72-88 in *A Labour of Love: Women, Work, and Caring,* edited by Janet Finch and Dulcie Groves. London: Routledge and Kegan Paul.

Chapter 4

1. Gross, Jane. 1996. "Friends in Sickness and Health." *Los Angeles Times,* June 19, pp. 1, 15.

2. Morris, Jenny. 1995. "Creating a Space for Absent Voices: Disabled Women's Experience of Receiving Assistance with Daily Living Activities." *Feminist Review* 51:68-93.

3. See Exhibit 4.1 on the low pay of paid caregivers.

4. Siddharthan, K., Ahern, M., and Rosenman, R. 1997. "The Impact of Ownership on Health Care Services in HMO's." *Health Manpower Management* 23:216-222; Jellinek, M., and Little, M. 1998. "Supporting Child Psychiatric Services Using Current Managed Care Approaches: You Can't Get There From Here." *Archives of Pediatrics and Adolescent Medicine* 15:323-326.

5. Diamond, Timothy. 1992. *Making Gray Gold: Narratives of Nursing Home Care.* Chicago: University of Chicago Press, p. 88.

6. Clarke-Stewart, Alison. 1993. *Daycare.* Rev. ed. Cambridge, MA: Harvard University Press. See also Scarr, S., and M. Eisenberg. 1993. "Child-Care Research: Issues, Perspectives and Results." *Annual Review of Psychology* 44:613-44.

7. Clarke-Stewart, 1993, op. cit.

8. Hooyman, Nancy R., and Judith Gonyea. 1995. *Feminist Perspectives on Family Care.* Newbury Park, CA: Sage.

9. The material on Sioux Falls is from Healy, 1996, op. cit., p. 12.

10. Hooyman and Gonyea, 1995, op. cit.

11. Gauthier, Anne Helene. 1996. *The State and the Family.* New York: Oxford University Press.

12. Diamond, 1992, op. cit., pp. 123-24.

13. Ibid., p. 13.

14. Ibid.

15. Ibid., p. 146.

16. Ibid., p. 4.

17. Brannon, Robert L. 1994. *Intensifying Care: The Hospital Industry, Professionalization, and the Reorganization of the Nursing Labor Process.* Amityville, NY: Baywood.

18. Shuit, Douglas P. 1996. "Hospital Nurses Feel Pain of Health System's Restructuring." *Los Angeles Times,* July 1, pp. A1, A19.

19. Murphy, Margaret. 1989. "Nursing Service Delivery Systems." Pp. 29-41 in *Nursing's Vital Signs: Shaping the Profession for the 1990s,* edited by the National Commission on Nursing Implementation Project. Battle Creek, MI: W. K. Kellogg Foundation.

20. Capitman, J. A. 1988. "Case Management for Long-Term and Acute Medical Care." *Health Care Financing Review* 10(annual suppl.):53-5.

21. Weitz, Rose, and Deborah A. Sullivan. 1990. "Licensed Lay Midwifery and Medical Models of Childbirth." Pp. 246-62 in *Circles of Care*, edited by Emily K. Abel and Margaret K. Nelson. Albany, NY: State University of New York Press; Candib, Lucy M. 1995. *Medicine and the Family: A Feminist Perspective.* New York: Basic Books.

22. Hooyman and Gonyea, 1995, op. cit., pp. 89-94.

23. Larson, Patricia J., and Marylin J. Dodd. 1991. "The Cancer Treatment Experience: Family Patterns of Caring." Pp. 61-78 in *Caring: The Compassionate Healer*, edited by Delores Gaut and Madeleine M. Leininger. New York: National League for Nursing Press; Tellis-Nayak, V., and Mary Tellis-Nayak. 1989. "Quality of Care and the Burden of Two Cultures: When the World of the Nurse's Aide Enters the World of the Nursing Home." *The Gerontologist* 29:307-13.

24. Diamond, 1992, op. cit., p. 17.

25. Scott, W. Richard. 1992. *Organizations.* 3d ed. Englewood Cliffs, NJ: Prentice Hall.

26. Foner, Nancy. 1994. *The Caregiving Dilemma: Work in the American Nursing Home.* Berkeley: University of California Press, p. 15.

27. Ibid., p. 18.

28. Ibid., p. 85.

29. Hooyman and Gonyea, 1995, op. cit.

30. Foner, 1994, op. cit., p. 83.

31. Sacks, Karen Brodkin. 1988. *Caring by the Hour.* Urbana, IL: University of Illinois Press.

32. Foner, 1994, op. cit., p. 38.

33. Ibid., p. 85.

34. Ibid., p. 39.

35. Ibid., p. 59.

36. Ibid., p. 61.

37. Ibid., p. 62.

38. Ibid.

39. Ibid.

40. Brannon, Robert. 1994. *Intensifying Care: The Hospital Industry, Professionalization, and the Reorganization of the Nursing Labor Process.* Amityville, NY: Baywood.

41. Subich, Linda M., Gerald V. Barrett, Dennis Doverspike, and Ralph A. Alexander. 1989. "The Effects of Sex-Role Related Factors on Occupational

Choice and Salary." Pp. 91-104 in *Pay Equity: Empirical Inquiries,* edited by Robert T. Michael, Heidi I. Hartmann, and Brigid O'Farrell. Washington, DC: National Academy Press.

42. Rosen, Ellen Israel. 1987. *Bitter Choices: Blue Collar Women in and out of Work.* Chicago: University of Chicago Press.

43. Huffman, Matt L. 1997. "When More Is Less: Sex Composition, Organizations and Earnings in U.S. Firms." *Work and Occupations* 24:214-244.

44. U.S. Bureau of the Census. 1998. *Current Population Reports.* Washington, DC: U.S. Government Printing Office, series p. 60. For international comparisons, see Reskin, Barbara, and Irene Padavic. 1994. *Women and Men at Work.* Newbury Park, CA: Pine Forge, p. 109.

45. U.S. Bureau of Labor Statistics. 1997. *Occupational Employment Statistics.* Retrieved May 5, 1998 from the World Wide Web: http://stats.bls.gov/oes/national/oes_serv.htm

46. England, Paula. 1992. *Comparable Worth: Theories and Evidence.* Hawthorne, NY: Aldine De Gruyter, p. 182.

47. U.S. Department of Labor, Bureau of Labor Statistics. 1998. Median Weekly Earnings of Full-Time Wage and Salary Workers by Selected Characteristics. Retrieved February 20, 1999 from the World Wide Web: http://www.bls.gov/opub/ted/1999/jan/wk4/art03.txt

48. Sacks, Karen Brodkin. 1990. "Does It Pay to Care?" Pp. 188-206 in *Circles of Care,* edited by Emily K. Abel and Margaret K. Nelson. Albany, NY: State University of New York Press.

49. Browner, Carole H., Kelly Ann Ellis, Theresa Ford, Joscelyn Silsby, Joanne Tampoya, and Cathy Yee. 1987. "Stress, Social Support, and Health of Psychiatric Technicians in a State Facility." *Mental Retardation* 25:31-8; Lundgren, Rebecka Inga, and Carole H. Browner. 1990. "Caring for the Institutionalized Mentally Retarded: Work Culture and Work-Based Social Support." Pp. 150-72 in *Circles of Care,* edited by Emily Abel and Margaret Nelson. Albany, NY: State University of New York Press.

50. Lundgren and Browner, 1990, op. cit., p. 156.

51. Ibid., p. 158.

52. Ibid., p. 157.

53. Ibid., p. 164.

54. In a personal communication to Francesca Cancian, Carole Browner confirmed that the licensing of psych techs probably contributed to their autonomy.

55. Lundgren and Browner, 1990, op. cit., p. 161.

56. Wesorick, Bonnie. 1991. "Creating an Environment in the Hospital Setting that Supports Caring via a Clinical Practice Model (CPM)."

Pp. 135-49 in *Caring: The Compassionate Healer,* edited by Delores A. Gaut and Madeleine M. Leininger. New York: National League for Nursing Press.

57. Ibid., p. 147.

58. Ibid., pp. 144-145.

59. Ibid., p. 146.

60. Gaut, Delores A., and Madeleine M. Leininger, eds. 1991. *Caring: The Compassionate Healer.* New York: National League for Nursing Press; Gaut, Delores A., ed. 1992. *The Presence of Caring in Nursing.* New York: National League for Nursing Press.

61. Silver, M. H. 1997. "Patients' Rights in England and the United States of America: The Patient's Charter and the New Jersey Patient Bill of Rights: A Comparison." *Journal of Medical Ethics* 23:213-20.

62. Melville, M. 1997. "Consumerism: Do Patients Have Power in Health Care?" *British Journal of Nursing* 6:337-40; Rodwin, Marc A. 1994. "Patient Accountability and Quality of Care: Lessons from Medical Consumerism and the Patients' Rights, Women's Health and Disability Rights Movements." *American Journal of Law and Medicine* 20:147-67.

63. Naples, Nancy. 1997. "The 'New Consensus' on the Gendered Social Contract: The 1987-88 US Congressional Hearings on Welfare Reform." *Signs* 22:907-45.

64. Morris, Jenny. 1993. *Independent Lives? Community Care and Disabled People.* Basingstoke, England: Macmillan; Mason, Philip. 1992. "The Representation of Disabled People: A Hampshire Centre for Independent Living Discussion Paper." *Disability, Handicap and Society* 7:79-84.

65. Morris, 1995, op. cit., p. 80.

66. Ibid., p. 88.

67. Ibid., pp. 85-86.

68. Ibid., p. 85.

Chapter 5

1. O'Hare, William P. 1996. "A New Look at Poverty in America." *Population Bulletin* 51(2):1-48.

2. Ibid.

3. Sainsbury, Diane. 1996. *Gender, Equality, and Welfare States.* Cambridge and New York: Cambridge University Press.

4. Tyack, David B. 1974. *The One Best System.* Cambridge, MA: Harvard University Press.

5. Becerra, Rosina, and Jeanne Giovannoni. 1979. *Defining Child Abuse.* New York: Free Press.

6. Benkov, Laura. 1994. *Reinventing the Family: Lesbian and Gay Parents.* New York: Crown Trade.

7. Page, Benjamin. 1983. *Who Gets What from Government.* Berkeley: University of California Press.

8. Dreier, Peter, and John Athens. 1996. "U.S. Housing Policy at the Crossroads." *Journal of Urban Affairs* 18(4):341-70.

9. Marmor, Theodore R., Jerry L. Mashaw, and Philip L. Harvey. 1990. *America's Misunderstood Welfare State.* New York: Basic Books; Edelman, Peter. 1997. "The Worst Thing Clinton Has Done." *The Atlantic Monthly,* March, pp. 43-58.

10. Nelson, Barbara J. 1990. "The Origins of the Two-Channel Welfare State." Pp. 123-51 in *Women, the State, and Welfare,* edited by Linda Gordon. Madison: University of Wisconsin Press.

11. Marmor et al., 1990, op. cit.; Edelman, 1997, op. cit.

12. Nelson, 1990, op. cit.; Marmor et al., 1990, op. cit.

13. Page, 1983, op. cit.

14. Abramovitz, Mimi. 1996. *Under Attack, Fighting Back.* New York: Monthly Review Press.

15. Marmor et al., 1990, op. cit.; Edelman, 1997, op. cit.

16. Abramovitz, 1996, op. cit.; Gordon, Linda. 1994. *Pitied But Not Entitled: Single Mothers and the History of Welfare 1890-1935.* New York: Free Press.

17. All material in this section and the next is available in both of two histories of welfare: Gordon, 1994, op. cit., and Skocpol, Theda. 1992. *Protecting Soldiers and Mothers.* Cambridge, MA: Harvard University Press.

18. Material in this section draws on Gordon, 1994, op. cit.

19. Orloff, Ann. 1993. "Gender and the Social Rights of Citizenship." *American Sociological Review* 58(3):303-28.

20. Gordon, 1994, op. cit.

21. Orloff, 1993, op. cit.

22. Abramovitz, 1996, op. cit.

23. Edelman, 1997, op. cit.

24. Ibid.

25. Ibid.

26. Oliker, Stacey. 1990. "Discourses on Motherhood in Welfare Reform." Presented at the annual meeting of the American Sociological Association, August 22, Washington, DC.

27. Oliker, Stacey J. 1995. "Work Commitment and Constraint Among Mothers on Workfare." *Journal of Contemporary Ethnography* 24(2):165-94.

28. Oliker, Stacey J. 1995. "The Proximate Contexts of Workfare and Work." *Sociological Quarterly* 36(2):251-72.

29. Ibid.; Oliker, 1995, "Work Commitment," op. cit.

30. Oliker, 1995, "Work Commitment," op. cit., p. 183.

31. Sainsbury, 1996, op. cit.; Gauthier, Anne Helene. 1996. *The State and the Family*. New York: Oxford University Press.

32. Marshall, T. H. 1950. *Citizenship and Social Class*. Cambridge: Cambridge University Press.

33. Sainsbury, 1996, op. cit.; Gauthier, 1996, op. cit.

34. Sainsbury, 1996, op. cit.

35. Gauthier, 1996, op. cit.; Navarro, Vicente. 1994. *The Politics of Health Policy*. Oxford: Blackwell.

36. Lewis, 1997, op. cit., p. 14.

37. Bussemaker, Jet, and Rian Voet. 1998. *Gender, Participation, and Citizenship in the Netherlands*. Aldershot: Ashgate; Hobson, Barbara. 1994. "Solo Mothers, Social Policy Regimes, and the Logics of Gender." Pp. 170-87 in *Gendering Welfare States*, edited by Diane Sainsbury. London: Sage; Lewis, Jane. 1997. *Lone Mothers in European Welfare Regimes*. London: Jessica Kingsley.

38. Bergmann, Barbara R. 1996. *Saving Our Children from Poverty*. New York: Russell Sage.

39. Ibid.

40. Material on Sweden draws on Sainsbury, 1996, op. cit.; Acker, Joan. 1994. "Women, Families, and Public Policy in Sweden." Pp. 33-50 in *Women, The Family, and Policy*, edited by Esther Ngan-ling Chow and Catherine White Berheide; Leira, Arnlaug. 1992. *Welfare States and Working Mothers*. Cambridge: Cambridge University Press.

41. Sainsbury, 1996, op. cit.

42. I have renamed concepts used by Hobson, 1994, op. cit.

43. Gordon, 1994, op. cit.

44. Young, Michael, and Peter Willmott. 1973. *The Symmetrical Family*. New York: Penguin.

45. Marcy Whitebook, of the Child Care Employees Project, Washington, DC, referred us to the Army case: U.S. Army Child Development Services. 1994. "A Staff Development and Compensation Initiative for Caregiving Personnel." Alexandria, VA: U.S. Army Child Development Services.

46. Ibid.

47. England, Paula. 1992. *Comparable Worth*. New York: Aldine de Gruyter; Steinberg, Ronnie J. 1990. "The Social Construction of Skill." *Work and Occupations* 17(4):449-82.

48. Sainsbury, 1996, op. cit.

Chapter 6

1. Fischer, Claude S., Robert M. Jackson, Ann Steuve, Katherine Gerson, and Lynn M. Jones. 1977. *Networks and Places.* New York: Free Press.

2. Ibid.

3. Ibid.; Wellman, Barry. 1979. "The Community Question." *American Journal of Sociology* 84:1201-31.

4. Wuthnow, Robert. ed. 1991. *Between States and Markets.* Princeton, NJ: Princeton University Press.

5. Bellah, Robert, Richard Madsen, William M. Sullivan, Ann Swidler, and Steven M. Tipton. 1985. *Habits of the Heart.* Berkeley: University of California Press.

6. Pardo, Mary. 1998. "Mexican American Women: Grassroots Community Activists." Pp. 251-62 in *Families in the U.S.,* edited by Karen Hansen and Anita Ilta Garvey. Philadelphia: Temple University Press. See also Naples, Nancy. 1998. *Grassroots Warriors.* New York: Routledge and Kegan Paul.

7. Wuthnow, Robert. 1995. *Learning to Care.* New York: Oxford University Press; Hodgkinson, Virginia A. 1995. "Key Factors Influencing Caring, Involvement, and Community." Pp. 21-50 in *Care and Community in Modern Society,* edited by Paul G. Schervish, Virginia A. Hodgkinson, Margaret Gates, and associates. San Francisco: Jossey-Bass.

8. Wuthnow, 1995, op. cit.; Hodgkinson, 1995, op. cit.

9. Wilson, John, and Marc Musick. 1997. "Who Cares? Toward an Integrated Theory of Volunteer Work." *American Sociological Review* 62:694-713.

10. Ibid.; Wuthnow, 1995, op. cit.

11. Wilson and Musick, 1997, op. cit.; Wuthnow, 1995, op. cit.

12. Wuthnow, 1995, op. cit., p. 162.

13. Sirianni, Carmen J., and Lewis A. Friedland. Forthcoming. *Civic Innovation in America.* Department of Sociology, Brandeis University, and School of Journalism and Mass Communication, University of Wisconsin.

14. Tronto, Joan C. 1993. *Moral Boundaries.* New York: Routledge.

15. Rochefort, David A. 1998. *From Poorhouses to Homelessness.* Westport, CT: Auburn; Torrey, E. Fuller. 1997. *Out of the Shadows.* New York: Wiley.

16. Rochefort, 1998, op. cit.; Torrey, 1997, op. cit.

17. Rochefort, 1998, op. cit.; Torrey, 1997, op. cit.

18. Kilborne, Peter. 1994. "Picking and Chosing Among the Truly Needy." *New York Times,* October 5, p. 3-4.

19. Dresang, Joel. 1998. "Food Charities Face Bigger Lead Under Wisconsin Works." *Milwaukee Journal-Sentinel,* July 21, p. 2; King, Dolores. 1998. "Study Reveals Rise of Hunger." *Boston Globe,* May 9, p. B1; Hernandez, Ramon. 1998. "Homeless Shelters Suffer as Welfare Rolls Decline." *New York Times,* January 14, p. 38; Hall, Ann. 1998. "Growing Numbers of Homeless." *Boston Globe,* Feb. 8, p. 11; Sullivan, Joe. 1998. "Putting All the Pieces Together." *U.S. Catholic* 63(7):30-5.

20. Rochefort, 1998, op. cit.; Torrey, 1997, op. cit.

21. Derus, Michele. 1998. "W-2 Families Squeeze in Together." *Milwaukee Journal-Sentinel,* January 18, p. F1.

22. Rochefort, 1998, op. cit.; Torrey, 1997, op. cit.

Chapter 7

1. See chapters 11 through 15 in Hooyman, Nancy R., and Judith Gonyea. 1995. *Feminist Perspectives on Family Care.* Thousand Oaks, CA: Sage.

2. Naples, Nancy. 1998. *Grassroots Warrior: Activist Mothering, Community Work, and the War on Poverty.* New York: Routledge.

3. Ibid.; Patterson, J. J. 1994. *America's Struggle Against Poverty: 1900-1994.* Cambridge, MA: Harvard University Press.

4. On Women Who Care and other groups representing specific care receivers, see Hooyman and Gonyea, 1995, op. cit., pp. 339-345. On grassroots organizing, see Naples, Nancy A., ed. 1998. *Community Activism and Feminist Politics: Organizing Across Race, Class and Gender.* New York: Routledge.

5. Hooyman and Gonyea, 1995, op. cit., p. 251.

6. Bailyn, Lotte. 1992. "Issues of Work and Family in Different National Contexts: How the United States, Sweden and Britain Respond." *Human Resource Management* 31:201-8; Lambert, S. J. 1993. "Workplace Policies as Social Policy." *Social Service Review* 67:237-60.

7. Hooyman and Gonyea, 1995, op. cit., p. 226.

8. Miller, Dorothy C. 1994. "What Is Needed for True Equality: An Overview of Policy Issues for Women." Pp. 27-56 in *Building on Women's Strengths,* edited by Lianne V. Davis. New York: Haworth.

9. Linsk, Nathan L., S. Keigher, L. Simon-Rusinowitz, and S. England. 1992. *Wages for Caring: Compensating Family Care of the Elderly.* New York: Praeger.

10. See chapter 5 in Coltrane, Scott. 1998. *Gender and Families.* Thousand Oaks, CA: Pine Forge Press.

11. Miller, 1994, op. cit.

Activism, 27
African-American experience, 19-21, 108
Aid to Families with Dependent
    Children (AFDC), 110, 111, 146-148
Army child care, 129-130, 156
Austria, 115-117, 116-117 (exhibits)

Biological perspective. *See* Natural
perspective
Breadwinner role, 21-23, 37-38, 109-111,
    115-116, 117
Bureaucracy, 72-73, 79-84, 122-123

Capitalism, 77-79, 107
Care receivers, 3, 10, 138, 141
    employment and, 64
    empowerment of, 98-99
    mutual caring, 58-59
    rights of, 97-98
    welfare recipients, 98
Caregiving, xiv, 2-3
    business support of, 155, 158
    devaluation of, 9-10, 24, 35, 87-91,
        151-152
    employment, hierarchies of, 34-35
    expansion of, 153-154
    gender-equalizing measures, 158-159
    gender links, 3-4
    natural perspective of, xii, 3, 4, 5-6, 8,
        38-39, 131, 156
    paid/unpaid, 136-137, 156-157
    separate spheres and, 8-9, 150-151
    social care, system of, 154-155
    status of, 129-130

value, recognition of/commitment
    to, 152-154
See also Family caring; Family
    patterns; Government policies;
    Historical context; Nursing
Carer/carer worker citizen policies,
    120-121
Caring, xi, 35
    defined, 2, 10-11
    good care, 3, 6
    patterns of, xiii
    social value of, 140-141
    See also Caregiving; Good care
Child care, 3, 9, 35, 117-118, 156
    Children's Bureau, 109
    family vs. day care, 45-48, 46 (exhibit)
    good care, 74-76
    government supported, 124
    United States Army program,
        129-130, 156
Childhood. *See* Family patterns
Citizens:
    carer/carer worker citizen policies,
        120-121
    political, 115
    social, 115, 140-141, 150
Clinical practice model of nursing, 95-96,
    122-123
Colonial American life, 14
    family care, 14-15
    fatherhood in, 17-18
    mothering in, 16-17
    religion and caregiving, 16-17
    trade in, 21
Community care, 135-136, 148

Aid to Families with Dependent
  Children (AFDC), 146-148
  benefits of, 137-141
  discrimination within, 142-143
  entitlements, 118
  gendered nature of, 143-145
  government programs, substitute
    for, 145-148
  innovations, needs-based, 140-141
  limitations of, 141-148
  mental illness in, 145-146, 147
  needs/resource imbalance, 141-142
  voluntary/paid care, 136-137
Comparable worth policies, 129-130
Couples, 58
  caring, methods of, 59-60
  male domination in, 60-62
  mutual caring, 58-59

Day care. *See* Child care
Demos, John, 14
Denmark, 116-117 (exhibits), 120
Devaluation:
  caring and, 9-10, 24
  emotional caring, 81, 85-87
  gendered caregiving, 151-152
  hands-on caregiving, 34-35
  housework and, 22-23
  paid caregiving, 72, 87-91
Divorce/custody laws, 103, 130, 133
Domesticity, 23-24, 108, 131-133

Education subsidies, 103
Elder care, 65-66, 68-69, 77-78
Emotional care:
  bureaucratizing of, 96-97
  devaluation of, 81, 85-87
  paid caregiving and, 94
  professionalizing of, 97-98
Employment:
  family caring and, 62-64, 65 (exhibit)
  motherhood and, 25-26, 62
Entitlements, universal, 118
European industrial nations, 102-103,
    114-115, 116-117 (exhibits), 153
  breadwinner-caregiver families,
    115-116, 117
  carer/carer worker citizen policies,
    120-121

conservative government welfare
    (Austria, France, Germany,
    Netherlands), 115-118, 116-117
    (exhibits)
  gender equity in caregiving, 120-121
  liberal/social democratic care
    (Scandinavian countries),
    116-117 (exhibits), 118-120, 131
  single-mother families, 116-117

Family and Medical Leave Act of 1993,
    103, 130
Family caring, 37-39, 38 (exhibit)
  chronic illness/disability and, 65-69
  day care vs., 45-48, 46 (exhibit)
  employment and, 62-64, 65 (exhibit)
  extended family network, 40-43
  government involvement in, 123-126
  male domestic care, 131-133, 154, 158
  nuclear families, 39
  nuclear ideal, inequality of, 43-45
  religion vs. government in, 126-127
  single-parent families, 39-40, 116-117,
    126
  social system of care, 154-155
  See also Community care; Couples;
    Parental care
Family patterns:
  African-American slaves and, 19-21
  colonial family care, 14-15
  industrial society, 21-27
  institutionalization of, 123-124, 126
  Native American care, 18-19
  separate spheres and, 8-9, 17-18
Family wage, 25
Feminism, 4, 8-9
Finland, 116-117 (exhibits), 120
France, 115, 116-117 (exhibits), 117-118

Gender, 1-2, 24
  caregiving and, xi, xiv, 3-4, 35,
    150-152
  community care and, 143-145
  couples, male domination in, 60-62
  equality in caregiving, 120-121,
    127-133, 154, 155, 157-159
  government policy and, 115, 127-133
  inequality of, 4, 10-11, 58, 121
  intimacy and, 61-62
  opportunities, equality in, 157-158

parenting and, 50-52, 53-54
spheres of, 26, 87-91
supports, equalizing, 118-119
welfare system and, 105-111
See also Caregiving; Natural
        perspective; Separate spheres
Germany, 115-117, 116-117 (exhibits)
Good care, 3, 6, 98
    bureaucracy and, 122-123, 127
    inequality and, 10-11
    nuclear ideal and, 43-45
    paid caregiving, 74-76
Government policies, 4-5, 101, 133-134,
    155
    Aid to Families with Dependent
        Children (AFDC), 110, 111,
        146-148
    bureaucratic impersonality, 122-123
    children's benefits, 102
    community care and, 139, 140
    comparable worth, 129-130
    cost control, 130
    elder care and, 68-69, 101-102
    entitlement/obligation to care,
        103-104
    Family and Medical Leave Act of
        1993, 103, 130
    family care and, 123-126
    gender equality and, 127-133, 158-159
    indirect provision, 104
    male domestic care and, 131-133, 158
    Medicare/Medicaid, 102
    New Deal, 109-111
    outside caregiving, 128
    regulating care, 103
    religious authority and, 126-127
    separate spheres and, 8-9, 115
    Sheppard-Towner Maternity and
        Infant Protection Act, 109
    single-parenting, realities of, 113-114
    Social Security, 102, 105, 106, 110, 124
    social services, 27, 64
    status of caregiving and, 129-130
    subsidies, 101-103
    welfare system, 105-114
    See also European industrial nations;
        Nursing homes; Paid caregiving;
        Welfare system

Health care industry:
    bureaucracy in, 72-73, 79-84, 96-97

cost cutting in, 78-79, 98
    experts and, 97, 98
    medical model of care, 79-81, 95
    See also Nursing; Nursing homes;
        Paid caregiving
Historical context, 7, 13-14, 35-36
    African-American slaves, 19-21
    colonial American life, 14-18
    industrial society, 21-27
    Native American care, 18-19
    nursing, professional caregiving,
        27-35
Housework, 22-23

Illness/disability, 65-69
Industrial society, 21
    breadwinner-caregiver family in,
        21-23
    gendered spheres in, 26
    motherhood, sentimental ideal,
        23-24, 25
    poverty in, 25-26, 28-29
    public activism, 27
Instinctual labor, xii, 4, 9, 151

Male domestic care, 131-133, 154, 158
Marriage law, 104
Maternalists, 108, 110, 112, 129
Medical model of care, 79-81, 95
Medicare/Medicaid, 102
Mental illness, deinstitutionalizing,
    145-146
Motherhood:
    colonial America and, 16-17
    employment vs., 25-26
    instinctual labor, xii, 4, 9, 151
    maternal instinct, 48-50
    natural perspective, 5-6, 8, 38-39, 131,
        156
    sentimental ideal of, 23-24, 25
    single, low-income, 113-114, 116-117,
        126
    socialization and, 52-54
    See also Family caring; Parental care;
        Welfare system
Mothers' pensions, 107-109, 110

Native American care, 18-19
Natural perspective, 5-6, 8, 38-39, 131, 156

Netherlands, 115-117, 116-117 (exhibits), 129
New Deal, 109-111
Nightingale, Florence, 29-30
Norway, 116-117 (exhibits), 120, 131
Nuclear:
    families, 39
    ideal, inequality of, 43-45, 70
Nursing, 3, 4, 10, 27-28
    aides, 76-77, 81, 94, 156
    autonomy in, 94, 95, 96
    clinical practice model of, 95-96
    emotional care, bureaucratizing of, 96-97
    gendered care and, 30-33
    healing, preindustrial, 28-29
    hierarchies in, 33-34, 82, 83-84
    professional status of, 29-31
    profits from caring, 77-79
    See also Paid caregiving
Nursing homes:
    bureaucracy in, 81-84
    emotional care, 81
    hierarchies of control, 84-87
    medical model of care and, 80
    profit industry, 77-79
    staffing shortages, 76-77

Older Women's League (OWL), 153

Paid caregiving, 71-72, 99-100
    authority and control, 73
    autonomy in, 94, 95, 96
    bureaucracy and, 72-73, 79-84, 91, 96-97
    care receivers and, 98-99
    devaluation of, 72, 81, 87-91
    emotional care, 94, 96-97
    experts and, 97, 98
    good care in, 74-76
    medical model of care, 79-81
    nursing homes, 76-79
    profit in, 77-79
    separate gendered spheres of, 87-91
    wages/value in, 89-91, 90 (exhibit)
    work culture in, case study, 92-95
    See also Health care industry; Nursing
Parental care:
    day care in, 45-48, 46 (exhibit)
    economic discrimination and, 57-58

male power and, 55-57
    maternal instincts, myth of, 48-50
    mothering/fathering, differences in, 50-52
    socialization of women, 52-55
Parent-worker benefits, 118-119
Personal assistants (PAs), 99
Policies. *See* Government policies
Political citizenship, 115
Poverty, 25-26, 28-29, 50, 104
Power relations, 10
    colonial parenting, 15
    couples, 60-62
    parenting and, 55-57
Professionalizing care:
    emotional care, 97-98
    experts and, 97
Profit, 72-73, 77-79
Psychiatric technicians, 92-95

Quality of care, 76
    emotional care, 81, 85-87, 94, 96-97
    staffing shortages, 76-77

Racism, 90-91, 108-109
Religion:
    caregiving and, 16-17, 18
    government policies and, 126-127

Sandwich generation, 4
Separate spheres, 8-9, 17-18, 21
    breadwinner-caregiver family, 21-23, 37-38, 110-111, 115-116, 117
    devaluation of caring, 87-91
    government policy and, 115
    motherhood, sentimental ideal, 23-24, 25
    nuclear ideal, inequality of, 43-45
    private/public, gendered, 26
    social services/charities, 27
    welfare, gender in, 107-111
    See also Gender
Sex roles. *See* Gender
Sheppard-Towner Maternity and Infant Protection Act, 109
Single mothers, 39-40, 112-114, 116-117, 126
Sioux Falls, SD, 74-75
Social care, system of, 154-155

Social citizenship, 115, 140-141, 150
Social hierarchies, 10
Social institutions, 7-8
    gendered spheres, 26, 87-91, 150-151
    social services/charities, 27
Social insurance programs, 105-106
Social Security Acts of 1935, 102, 105, 106, 124
Sociological perspective, 1, 3, 6-7
    motherhood vs. employment, 25-26
    separate spheres, 8-9
    social institutions in, 7-8
    See also Historical context
Spheres. *See* Separate spheres
Sweden, 116-117 (exhibits), 118-119, 129, 131

Ulrich, Lauren, 16
United States Army child care, 129-130, 156

Value. *See* Wages/value

Wages/value, 25, 89-91, 90 (exhibit), 129-130, 150-151, 152-154
Welfare system, 98, 104, 105
    Aid to Families with Dependent Children, 110, 111, 146-148
    breadwinner-caregiver ideal and, 110-111
    Children's Bureau, 109
    end of, 111-113, 146-148
    inequalities in, 106-107, 109-111
    mothers' pensions, 107-109, 110
    New Deal and, 109-110
    public assistance, 106
    separate gendered spheres, 107-111
    single-mother caregiving, invisibility of, 112-114, 126
    social insurance programs, 105-106
    Social Security Acts of 1935, 110
Wesorick, Bonnie, 95-96, 97
Women:
    caregivers, xi, xiii, 3-5, 69
    colonial mothering, 16-17
    domesticity of, 23-24, 108
    housework, devaluation of, 22-23, 156
    inequality of, xii, 4, 10-11
    men, social equality with, 131-133
    motherhood vs. employment, 25-26, 62
    public activism, 27
    See also Gender; Natural perspective; Nursing
Women Who Care, 153
Work culture, 92-95
Workfare, 4-5